S

IS FOR

STUPID

D0071490

Other Books by Leland Gregory

S IS FOR STUPID

An Encyclopedia of Stupidity

Leland Gregory

**Andrews McMeel
Publishing, LLC**
Kansas City • Sydney • London

S Is for Stupid copyright © 2011 by Leland Gregory. All rights reserved.
Printed in the United States of America. No part of this book may be used or
reproduced in any manner whatsoever without written permission except in
the case of reprints in the context of reviews.

Andrews McMeel Publishing, LLC
an Andrews McMeel Universal company
1130 Walnut Street, Kansas City, Missouri 64106

11 12 13 14 15 RR2 10 9 8 7 6 5 4 3 2 1

ISBN: 978-1-4494-0062-0

Library of Congress Control Number: 2010929346

www.andrewsmcmeel.com

Attention: Schools And Businesses
Andrews McMeel books are available at quantity discounts with bulk purchase
for educational, business, or sales promotional use. For information, please
e-mail the Andrews McMeel Publishing Special Sales Department:
specialsales@amuniversal.com

contents

advertising

According to a November 23, 1995, *Los Angeles Times* article, the Oakland Ballet withdrew a billboard advertising campaign showing two ballet dancers in tutus after receiving a complaint. It wasn't the image that was the problem; it was the slogan: "Go ahead—take another date to miniature golf and die a virgin. Oakland Ballet. You might just like it." One of the ads appeared across the street from a local high school, where the assistant principal claimed it sent the wrong message to teenagers by "suggesting [that] being a virgin is bad."

Here's a list of names of Japanese automobiles as they appeared in English on each vehicle at a Tokyo trade show. The list was compiled by John Phillips and appeared in his *Car and Driver* column in February 1996:

- Mitsubishi Mini Active Urban Sandal
- Subaru Gravel Express
- Mazda Bongo Friendlee
- Daihatsu Rugger Field Sports Resin Top
- Nissan Prairie Joy
- Suzuki Every Joy Pop Turbo
- Mitsubishi Delica Space Gear Cruising Active
- Subaru Sambar Dias Astonish!!
- Isuzu Mysterious Utility Wizard
- Daihatsu Town Cube
- Nissan Big Thumb Harmonized Truck
- Isuzu Giga 20 Light Dump

A

advertising

In December 1996, computer giant Microsoft translated its name as "we ruan" for its Japanese operation. It wasn't well received by most Japanese men because the translation literally means "small and soft."

The last televised cigarette ad, a commercial for Virginia Slims, was aired on *The Tonight Show* on December 31, 1970. Cigarette advertising was banned from both radio and television effective January 1, 1971.

agriculture

In 1981, the Reagan administration declared that ketchup could "be counted as one of the two vegetables required as part of the school lunch program." And according to the U.S. Department of Agriculture under the George W. Bush administration in 2004, "Batter-coated French fries are a fresh vegetable." Thanks to the government fries and ketchup, our kids are finally eating healthy.

A

agriculture

In February 1996, the Senate passed a groundbreaking farm bill that would eliminate a lot of nonsensical federal subsidies for farmers (for example, mohair production, squash subsidies, and so on). But planted deep in the furrows of the farm bill was a little attachment to create yet another committee, the U.S. Popcorn Board. This board's job is to promote this lighter-than-air snack that has been doing extremely well, especially after the FDA scared theaters into using canola oil. Senate Agriculture Committee chairman Richard G. Lugar (R-IN) had the kernel of an idea for the Popcorn Board with help from the Popcorn Institute, a trade association. The following are excerpts from Section 901 and 902 (a) 1–4 of the Popcorn Act.

Subtitle A—Popcorn

SEC. 901. SHORT TITLE

This subtitle may be cited as the "Popcorn Promotion, Research, and Consumer Information Act."

SEC. 902. FINDINGS AND DECLARATIONS OF POLICY.

    (a) FINDINGS—Congress finds that:

        (1) popcorn is an important food that is a valuable part of the human diet;

(2) the production and processing of popcorn plays a significant role in the economy of the United States in that popcorn is processed by several popcorn processors, distributed through wholesale and retail outlets and consumed by millions of people throughout the United States and foreign countries;

(4) the maintenance and expansion of existing markets and uses and the developments of new markets and uses for popcorn are vital to the welfare of processors and persons concerned with marketing, using, and producing popcorn for the market, as well as to the agricultural economy of the United States.

What's next—the U.S. Milk Dud, Cracker Jack, and Goobers Board?

The U.S. Department of Agriculture once spent $46,000 to calculate how long it takes to cook eggs.

A | airplanes

September 11, 2001, changed the way airlines do business and what passengers can carry on board, but for some, the changes have yet to sink in. According to a September 13, 2009, *New York Post* article, so far that year, the Transportation Security Administration had confiscated 123,189 items from passengers—and that was just from the three main airports serving New York City (JFK, La Guardia, and Newark). Included were 43 explosives, 1,602 knives, a shower rod, rodeo whips, a ten-point set of deer antlers, several fire extinguishers, a tree branch, nunchakus, a grill, a baby alligator, "unwashed adult toys," a gassed-up chainsaw, a six-foot African spear, and a kitchen sink.

A woman called a travel agent and asked, "Do airlines put your physical description on your bag so they know whose luggage belongs to who?"

The agent replied, "No, why do you ask?"

The timid-sounding woman said, "Well, when I checked in with the airline, they put a tag on my luggage that said FAT, and I'm overweight. Is there any connection?"

After putting her on hold for a minute while she regained her composure, the agent explained to the woman that the city code for Fresno is FAT, and that the airline was just putting a destination tag on her luggage.

Makes you wonder: If the woman saw the word "terminal" on her luggage, would she think she was really sick?

alcohol

On March 27, 2003, the *Boulder (CO) Daily Camera* reported that a thirty-nine-year-old driver from Boulder had accidentally crashed into a tree after celebrating his car's odometer hitting one hundred thousand miles with a bottle of champagne.

STUPID

"Intoxicated persons are prohibited from operating a vehicle on any public highway or street, except for a wheelbarrow."

—UTAH ORDINANCE

The U.S. House of Representatives added $5.6 million to the 2006 federal budget for the Ernest Gallo Clinic and Research Center (EGCRC), which, according to its Web site, "was established in 1980 to study basic neuroscience and the effects of alcohol and drug abuse on the brain." This earmark was buried in the defense budget even though the EGCRC never mentions anything related to defense research. But who's going to wine over a few million anyway?

Robert Lee Brock, an inmate at the Indian Creek Correctional Center in Chesapeake, Virginia, filed a $5 million lawsuit against himself. Brock claimed that Brock violated his religious beliefs and his civil rights by forcing himself to get himself drunk—and because of this self-induced drunkenness, he perpetrated several crimes. Brock, who is serving twenty-three years for breaking and entering and grand larceny, wrote, "I partook of alcoholic beverages in 1993, July 1, as a result I caused myself to violate my religious beliefs. This was done by my going out and getting arrested." He went on to claim, "I want to pay myself $5 million [for violating my own rights] but ask the state to pay it in my behalf since I can't work and am a ward of the state."

Judge Rebecca Beach Smith dismissed the claim in April 1995.

alcohol

A

alcohol

"Whoever operates an automobile or motorcycle on any public way—laid out under authority of law recklessly or while under the influence of liquor shall be punished; thereby imposing upon the motorist the duty of finding out at his peril whether certain highways had been laid out recklessly or while under the influence of liquor before driving his car over them."

—Massachusetts state ordinance

According to an October 24, 2008, article in the *Lexington (KY) Herald-Leader*, and TheSmokingGun.com's public records search engine, fifty-eight-year-old Henry Earl of Lexington, Kentucky, has been arrested 1,333 times, mostly for public intoxication.

alcohol

Police confronted Erik Salmons in Copley Township, Ohio, after receiving complaints that he was intoxicated and annoying customers in a local restaurant. They decided not to arrest him but did insist that he call someone to pick him up, and Salmons agreed. Once at home, however, Salmons decided that being accused of being intoxicated was insulting, and he drove to police headquarters to demand a Breathalyzer test to clear his name. According to an April 7, 2009, *Akron Beacon Journal* article, police agreed to Salmons's request and promptly arrested him once the results were in.

Arrested on charges of drug possession, driving while intoxicated, and driving without a license:
Mr. Fred Flintstone.

—*Lewisville (TX) Leader*, February 14, 2005

According to an October 21, 2003, report on KNBC-TV in Los Angeles, a taste test turned violent in Pomona, California, when James Howle and Kevin Williams stabbed each other in a disagreement over which of their two alcoholic drinks tasted better.

An unnamed forty-four-year-old Dutch motorist from Krommenie, Netherlands, astonished traffic police because he had drunk so much alcohol that he crashed their Breathalyzer test. At first, the machine refused to work and then showed that the unidentified man's level was out of range. According to a May 26, 2003, article on Ananova.com, police performed a blood test on the man, who claimed to have had only "four beers." The results of that test showed that he was seven times over the legal limit. The man was later sentenced to a fifteen-month driving ban, a $345 fine, and a two-week suspended jail sentence.

alligators

What's the difference between an alligator and a crocodile? Most people would answer that an alligator has a wide U-shaped rounded snout whereas crocodiles have longer, more pointed, V-shaped noses. But David Havenner of Port Orange, Florida, would say the difference between the two is that an alligator is something you can use to hit your girlfriend. Havenner was arrested after throwing beer cans at Nancy Monico and then slapping her with a live three-foot alligator he kept in their mobile home. In a July 17, 2004, Associated Press article, Havenner said he resorted to this reptilian behavior because Monico had angrily bit his hand when she discovered there was no beer left in the trailer.

"ALLIGATOR EATS COCKER SPANIEL"

—*Tampa Tribune* headline, October 10, 2005

Members of the Georgia state game commission were fiercely debating the pros and cons of regulating "alligator rides" when one alert member noticed a typographical error on the agenda—the commission was actually supposed to be discussing whether they should regulate alligator *hides*.

the amish

A police officer in Middlefield, Ohio, spotted a vehicle heading down a stretch of road with the driver fast asleep. The officer gave chase while trying to get the driver to wake up and regain control of the vehicle. The police officer didn't turn on his siren, though, because he didn't want to spook the horse. You see, the driver was a seventeen-year-old Amish boy and the vehicle was his horse-drawn carriage. The officer blocked the road with his cruiser, and the horse, buggy, and rider all careened into a ditch. The horse was slightly injured but made a full recovery. The boy was charged with driving under the influence.

A drag race on a country road south of Fort Wayne, Indiana, took a bad turn when one of the drivers lost control and caused a head-on collision, leaving one woman with a head injury. According to the April 14, 2003, *Indianapolis Star* article, what makes this story unique is that the drag race was between two Amish horse-drawn buggies. The driver of a third buggy, David Wickey, was arrested on charges of driving while intoxicated.

art

In January 2006, artist Trevor Corneliusien told sheriff's deputies that while camping in California's Mojave Desert he had shackled his ankles together in order to draw a picture of his legs. After he had finished his sketch he realized he didn't have the key to the lock and had to hop around the desert for nearly twelve hours before finding his way to a gas station.

London artist Gavin Turk sold an ordinary empty cardboard box, the size of a typical moving box, for $16,000 at a Christie's auction, according to the September 2, 2009, edition of the *New York Post*. The article went on to explain that the box was actually a sculpture designed to look exactly like an ordinary empty cardboard box.

I n 1994, artist Zhang Huan performed *12 Square Meters* in Beijing, China. The performance consisted of him lathering "his nude body in honey and fish oil" and exposing himself to "swarming flies and insects."

S telios Arcadious, better known as Stelarc, a Greek Australian performance artist, had a laboratory-grown ear surgically implanted onto his left forearm as an "augmentation of the body's form." According to an October 11, 2007, *Daily Mail* article, Stelarc said that although the ear doesn't function, he plans, for his next exhibit, to install a tiny microphone in it and connect it to a Bluetooth transmitter, thus allowing patrons to hear what his ear does or doesn't hear.

Chilean Danish artist Marco Evaristti presented *Helena: The Goldfish Blender*, in 2000. The display consisted of a series of blenders, each one containing live goldfish. Museumgoers were invited to turn on the appliances and thereby blend the goldfish.

New York artist Ariana Page Russell, who refers to herself as the "human Etch A Sketch," suffers from a skin disorder called dermatographism, which creates itchy raised red welts at the slightest scratch. Russell now "skin draws" on herself and offers photographs for sale. According to an April 13, 2009, article in the *Daily Telegraph*, Russell must work quickly as the welts remain for less than an hour.

A automobiles

STUP ID

"Motorists may not back their automobiles into trees in public places."

—Princeton, New Jersey, ordinance

"I think where he was was the worst possible place to be," said the medical director of the Queensland Ambulance Service in Australia. He was talking about the most unfortunate of the six passengers who were injured in a rear-end collision between a Ford Festiva and a larger car. So how can you fit six people in a tiny Festiva? You put one of them in the trunk, according to the *Brisbane Courier-Mail*. "It's literally too stupid for words," said a spokesman for the Royal Automobile Club of Queensland. "But we do feel bad for the man."

STUP ID

"No one shall drive any kind of motorized vehicle while said vehicle is running while dipping snuff or chewing tobacco."

—McAlester, Oklahoma, ordinance

"TEXT-MESSAGING DRIVER HITS PARKED PATROL CAR"

—*Arizona Republic* HEADLINE, JUNE 27, 2007

automobiles

Shoppers at the Smith's Food and Drug store in Albuquerque, New Mexico, say they spotted a man in the parking lot with his pants around his ankles, "humping" the back end of his own car while screaming and flailing his arms around. According to an August 13, 2009, report on KRQU-TV, police arrived to find forty-six-year-old Danny Brawner asleep next to the car. When they awoke him he appeared intoxicated. Brawner was arrested and charged with one count of indecent exposure and two counts of aggravated indecent exposure (a fourth-degree felony because children were present during his auto-erotic act).

A

automobiles

In Pennsylvania, "Any motorist driving along a country road at night must stop every mile and send up a rocket signal, wait 10 minutes for the road to be cleared of livestock, and then continue." The statute goes on to declare: "Any motorist who sights a team of horses coming toward him must pull well off the road, cover his car with a blanket or canvas that blends with the country-side, and let the horses pass. If the horses appear skittish, the motorist must take his car apart, piece by piece, and hide it under the nearest bushes."

"WOMAN WAS TEACHING BOY, 11, TO DRIVE WHEN SHE WAS RUN OVER"

—*Salt Lake Tribune* HEADLINE, JUNE 11, 2009

Stephen Thomas Manley, Jr., was driving down Farm Road 920 north of Weatherford, Texas, when a car driven by B. J. Justin Lundin began tailgating him. Manley tapped his brakes to get Lundin to back off, an action that apparently enraged the twenty-year-old Poolville, Texas, native. According to an article in the *Fort Worth Star-Telegram*, Lundin passed Manley on the night of January 6, 2003, and then blocked his car by stopping in front of it. Lundin jumped out of his car and began throwing rocks at Manley. He was in the process of kicking and hitting Manley's car when another car drove by and ran him over, killing him instantly.

STUPID

"Two vehicles which are passing each other in opposite directions shall have the right of way."

—NEW YORK STATE VEHICLE AND TRAFFIC LAW, ARTICLE 6, PARAGRAPH 82, SUBSECTION DIVISION 3

"POLICE: MAN RUNS OVER WIFE AFTER 'WHO DRIVES' SPAT"

—*FLORIDA TODAY* HEADLINE, FEBRUARY 22, 2008

A lead-footed motorist was caught by a high-speed camera that photographed his car's license plate and recorded his speed. When police mailed the speeder his sixty-five-dollar ticket, they included the photograph that was imprinted with the date and speed. In response, the motorist mailed them a photograph of a check. Not wanting the photograph wars to develop any further, the police mailed the man a picture of a pair of handcuffs. He got the picture, in more ways than one, and immediately sent them a check for the full amount.

The following are actual statements given by insurance policyholders describing automobile accidents in which they were involved.

"The accident occurred when I was attempting to bring my car out of a skid by steering into the other vehicle."

"I was driving my car out the driveway in the usual manner, when it was struck by the other car in the same place it had been struck several times before."

"I was on my way to the doctor's with rear-end trouble when my universal joint gave way causing me to have an accident."

"As I approached the intersection, a stop sign suddenly appeared in a place where no stop sign had ever appeared before. I was unable to stop in time to avoid the accident."

"MAN BLAMES RECKLESS DRIVING ON MARTIANS"

—Reuters headline, January 2, 2003

According to a May 29, 2009, article in the *Santa Monica Daily Press*, a fifty-six-year-old woman in Santa Monica, California, was killed when she left her stalled car in drive while she crawled underneath to determine why it wouldn't start. She accidentally triggered the starter with a screwdriver, and the car drove over her.

banks

Police in Indianapolis arrested Fifth Third Bank manager Dwayne Roberts and charged him with arson and theft. Roberts, in an attempt to hide his acts of embezzlement, had started a fire inside the bank's vault in order to make it impossible to determine how much money had been stolen. He closed and locked the vault and quickly discovered that he had left his keys inside. According to a May 12, 2009, article in the *Indianapolis Star*, Roberts was also unable to lock the bank's doors or drive home.

B

banks

William W. Bresler, Jr., was arrested for attempted robbery of a National City Bank in Westerville, Ohio, but instead of being taken to jail he was taken in for a psychiatric evaluation. According to a March 19, 2003, article in the *Westerville News*, Bresler had demanded the teller hand over exactly one penny.

In Dothan, Alabama, a wanted bank robber who had successfully eluded police was finally captured when he was arrested committing another crime—shoplifting an eighty-nine-cent carton of orange juice.

The timing was off for a bank robber in Cheshire, Massachusetts. He pulled off the heist at 4:30 p.m. and tried to make his getaway through downtown North Adams. He got stuck in rush-hour traffic and was apprehended by an officer on foot.

banks

A man accused of robbing $3,000 from a New Jersey bank filed a $1.2 million defamation lawsuit against the bank teller he apparently robbed. The alleged bank robber filed his suit from prison, where he was awaiting trial. The suit claims that the teller defamed and slandered him by telling police he had threatened to shoot her if she didn't hand over the money. The accused robber said he was deeply hurt by her slanderous words because, he claims, he never threatened to shoot her and simply handed her a very polite note that read, "I want the money now."

What, no "please"?

When a teller in Swansea, Massachusetts, told a would-be bank robber she had no money, he fainted. He was still unconscious when the police arrived. When officers found his getaway car they discovered the keys were locked inside it.

B

banks

Jason Durant, a novice bank robber, successfully robbed the National Iron Bank in New Milford, Connecticut, and escaped with an undisclosed amount of cash. He ran behind the bank building to make his getaway, accidently lost his footing, and tumbled down a steep hill. During his head-over-heels roll, Durant lost control of the bank bags and his gun and managed to break his leg in several places. But that's not all, according to an April 30, 2009, article in the *Waterbury (CT) Republican-American*. Durant then smashed into a plow blade, leaving him with an enormous gash and only two dollars from the robbery money. When he showed up bloodied and bruised at the hospital, a suspicious staff member notified police and he was arrested.

Trying to make a clean sweep, a man in Calgary, Alberta, robbed a Bank of Nova Scotia armed only with a bottle of household cleaner.

"This is a bank robbery
of the Federal Reserve Bank
of Dallas, Texas. Give me
all the money.

Thank you,
Ronnie Darnell Bell."

—NOTE FOUND ON ALLEGED INTENDED BANK ROBBER
RONNIE DARNELL BELL

B

We all know the scene in the movies where the would-be robber sticks his finger in his pocket and pretends it's a gun, right? Well, apparently one robber thought that was a good idea and tried it out in an attempt to rob the Bank of America in Merced, California. But he forgot one thing—to hide his finger in his pocket. The index-indicating idiot aimed his uncovered finger—with his thumb cocked, of course—at the teller demanding money. The teller asked the robber to wait, then walked away. After some time the bank robber got tired of waiting. He unloaded his finger and walked out of the bank and across the street to another bank. This time he tried a different approach. He leaped over the counter and tried to wrestle a cash drawer key from a teller. An employee grabbed the key and told the thwarted thief to "get out of there," according to Sergeant Gary Austin. The two-time loser was arrested shortly thereafter when he was discovered sitting in a clump of nearby shrubs.

I guess now every time he sticks his finger up his nose it can be considered a suicide attempt.

bicycles

The February 23, 1992, "Police Report" column of the *Kerrville (TX) Daily Times* described the following confrontation: A Kerrville police officer arrested a twenty-three-year-old man for assault after he allegedly tried to gore the off-duty officer with the deer antlers he had strapped to the handlebars of his bicycle.

B

bicycles

A September 10, 2010, *San Francisco Chronicle* article reported that a sheriff's deputy was called to a gas station in Stuart, Florida, on a report of a man having an "obscene argument." When they arrived, they found a "very intoxicated" sixty-eight-year-old Richard Bialon arguing with his bicycle. "Customers were coming to the Mobil and were very disturbed as to the yelling," the police report noted. The report didn't state what the "argument" was about or what roll the bicycle had in the confrontation. Bialon was arrested for disorderly intoxication. No word on the punishment for the bike.

"DEFENDANT STOLE BICYCLE TO GET TO COURT ON TIME"

—*Guardian* HEADLINE, JUNE 13, 2006

A seventy-seven-year-old Jacksonville, Florida, man decided to help out his busy daughter by riding his bicycle to Long Branch Elementary School to pick up his four-year-old grandson. When he arrived back home, instead of getting an "Atta boy" from his daughter, he got a "Who's that boy?" The grandfather had picked up a boy and put him on his bike without ever realizing he had the wrong child. According to a November 8, 2007, report, the mother of the boy who was accidentally taken exclaimed, "[The two boys] don't even look alike."

A bicycle bandit peddled his bike to the drive-through window at a Fort Worth, Texas, Taco Bell and placed his order. He wanted all the money in the store . . . and a chalupa.

B

bicycles

The owner of a Ford Probe was waiting at a traffic light when a man came out of nowhere, put a knife to his throat, demanded the car, pushed the owner out, and drove away. The car thief got only a short distance away when he collided with a pickup truck and totaled the car. Now he knew he was really in trouble—not only had he stolen a car but now he was involved in a hit-and-run. The criminal quickly looked around for another mode of transportation and found a hot little pink and white number and took off. When the police apprehended him, he claimed he was the rightful owner of the set of wheels and was simply on his way home. The police doubted the man's explanation because his new getaway vehicle was a little girl's bicycle. The man was caught furiously peddling away from the scene and was charged with, among other things, two counts of larceny—one for the car and one for the bike. Look, ma . . . no brains.

the blind

The Texas Commission for the Blind, whose sole responsibility is to supply support for the visually impaired in the workplace, was charged by the U.S. Department of Justice with discrimination. The commission was found guilty of issuing printed employee manuals but not making available Braille or large-type versions for its sight-impaired workers. They were forced to pay $55,000 to settle the claims. So the commission was both: out of sight and out of mind.

B

the blind

A Columbus, Ohio, criminal thought he had found the perfect person to rob—heck; he wouldn't even have to wear a mask. The robber knew only one thing about his victim: that he was blind. He didn't know he was also a state wrestling champion. When the robber tried to strong-arm his victim, he found himself flipping through the air, being slammed roughly to the ground, and then held in a half nelson until police arrived.

Guess he should have wrestled a bit more with his decision whether to commit the crime.

A uthorities searched the home of a former U.S. Forest Service employee and uncovered truckloads of stolen merchandise, including ready-to-eat meals, tent straps, conference room furniture, and a five-thousand-watt generator. The man claimed he had an impairment that rendered him innocent of the charges. Did he claim kleptomania, multiple-personality syndrome, amnesia, the heartbreak of psoriasis? Nope. The man claimed he was too blind to realize he had actually stolen that much stuff.

His written excuse to Judge William Polly stated, "During the years of working for the Forest Service, I was conditioned to think it was customary practice to borrow and take excess government items. Due to my visual impairment, I didn't realize I had so many items on my property to be returned."

Polly, however, could see right through the man's poor eyesight excuse. "The evidence is absolutely overwhelming that he stole many, many things which far exceeded any mistake or oversight," the judge said. "He greatly abused the job and trust that was placed in him."

B the border

U.S. Border Patrol officers are upset by their new uniforms; it's not that they're not fashionable or difficult to accessorize—it's that they're made in Mexico. A spokesman for U.S. Customs and Border Protection, now under the control of the Department of Homeland Security, complained that the uniforms, although purchased from a U.S. vendor, had work outsourced to other countries. "Sometimes, certain plants will do the cutting and send it off to other plants for assembling," said spokesman Jim Mitchie in June 2004. "So, what's going on where, I can't tell you."

As long as they don't mix stripes with polka dots and don't wear white shoes after Labor Day, I think everything will be fine.

"But we've got a big border in Texas, with Mexico, obviously—and we've got a big border with Canada— Arizona is affected."

—George W. Bush, Washington, D.C., June 24, 2004

I need to look at my map again because either Arizona has shifted north or Canada has invaded.

During times of turmoil and civil unrest in foreign countries, the United States always tries to help in some way or another: food, clothes, weapons—whatever it takes to help out the underdog. So it was business as usual in 1994 when the United States dropped relief supplies to Rwandan refugees during an emergency mission. A simple throw of the lever would release much-needed supplies—but the lever was thrown a little late. Seventeen tons of corned beef, flour, and other foods bombarded the refugees, who had to take cover from this "supplies strike." A UN helicopter and a school were nearly destroyed, and several Rwandans were injured, but nobody was killed, so this story had a good ending.

A similar story had a bad ending. Shortly after the Persian Gulf War, the United States dropped pallets of supplies to aid Kurdish refugees on the border of Turkey and Iraq. The planes missed their drop-off spot and crushed eight Kurds to death.

bullets

Warren County, New York, deputies were called to investigate a shooting in Lake Luzerne, New York, on the evening of May 12, 2007. When they arrived, they found the victim, Damion Mosher, had sustained a wound in his abdomen from a .223-caliber bullet. Even though the deputies weren't from the vice squad they quickly discovered that the perpetrator was—a vise. Mosher had been discharging the bullets by clamping them in a steel vise, putting a screwdriver on the primer, and striking the screwdriver with a hammer so he could sell the brass shell casings for scrap (which goes for $1.70 a pound). Mosher was on his nearly one hundredth bullet when he lost the final round to a round.

A .22-caliber bullet wounded Chaddrick Dickson of Monroe, Louisiana, after he repeatedly slammed it on the ground. According to an article from the December 30, 2001, edition of the *Seattle Times*, Dickson claimed he wanted to remove the gunpowder from the casing because he planned to mix it into his dog's food in order to make the animal meaner.

A scientist in Atlanta collected more than ten pounds of shell casings from the city's streets during lunch hours. The casings ranged from .22-caliber bullets to AK-47 assault rifle ammunition. Commenting on the scientist's collection, police officials in Atlanta said that didn't necessarily mean the city isn't safe. Perhaps, they said, people were firing their weapons elsewhere and leaving the shells in Atlanta. Now that's a long shot.

Eric Fortune of Ashtabula County, Ohio, had been nagging his brother to shoot him in the leg because he always wondered what it would feel like to be shot. His brother finally got tired of the constant pleading and, according to a March 31, 2009, article in the *Ashtabula Star Beacon*, finally agreed to shoot his brother in the leg. Fortune was rushed to the Ashtabula County Medical Center for his gunshot wound. It was so painful he couldn't describe what it felt like; he could only cry.

Howard Sheppard of Deltona, Florida, found some bullets on the ground and wanted to see what would happen if he struck one with a metal punch. The result, according to a January 10, 2009, *Daytona Beach News-Journal* article, was that he was shot in the arm and had to be taken to Florida Hospital DeLand.

On July 29, 2008, WCCO-TV in Minneapolis reported on police chief Tim Dolan's speech honoring SWAT officers for their bravery and expert handing of a December 2007 middle-of-the-night raid of a house that reportedly contained a gang's guns. What's shocking about the chief's praise of his team is that they raided the wrong house. The occupants, surprised at the no-knock entrance, began shooting at the officers, who returned fire.

"The easy decision would have been to retreat [but the] team did not take the easy way out," Dolan bragged. Fortunately no one was hit but the house was riddled with bullets. The chief later apologized for the mistake but defended his team's actions by saying it was "a perfect example of a situation that could have gone horribly wrong, but did not because of the [team's] professionalism."

B

bullets

An August 2000 workplace brawl in Irvine, California, turned fatal when one man grabbed another in a headlock and put a gun to his head. The man firing the gun shot his victim in the face—but the victim wasn't the one who died. The bullet passed through the man's cheek and lodged deep into the shooter's own chest, killing him. This guy went from giving a headlock to getting a headstone.

canines | C

A fter a dog bit and flattened the tire of a young neighbor girl's bicycle, a Cumberland County, North Carolina, sheriff's deputy was dispatched to investigate. When the deputy arrived, she didn't find the dog, the bicycle, or the little girl and decided to drive to the dog owner's house to get more information on the incident. When she parked her cruiser in the driveway, the family dog promptly ran out and attacked the car's tires. All four of the cruiser's tires were bitten and flattened, but no charges were filed. "The dog didn't try to attack the deputy," a department spokeswoman said. "He just doesn't like tires."

STUPID

"No dog shall be in public without its master on a leash."

—STRANGELY PHRASED BELVEDERE, CALIFORNIA,
ORDINANCE

C

canines

In July 1996, Raymondville, Texas, attorney
Juan Guerra, representing Alex Alzaldua, filed
a $25,000 lawsuit against Dennis Hickey. The
lawsuit alleged that while at Hickey's home,
Alzaldua had suffered injuries when he "suddenly
without warning" tripped over Hickey's dog
in the kitchen. According to Guerra, Alzaldua
should have been warned that he was "walking
on the floor at his own risk" and of "the dog's
propensity of lying in certain areas."

On February 26, 2004, a deputy tried to stop thirty-seven-year-old Girlamo Marinello of Shelby Township, Michigan, for running a stop sign in Oakland Township. Marinello rammed the deputy's car and then got out of his vehicle and started swinging—not his fists, but a four-pound French toy poodle on a leash. According to a January 17, 2005, article in the *Detroit Free Press*, Marinello was charged with animal cruelty, assault with intent to do great bodily harm, fleeing and eluding while causing a collision, and carrying concealed weapons (knives found in the truck—not the poodle). The state forensic psychiatry center found Marinello not criminally responsible, and the poodle was put up for adoption.

> "Females in heat must be properly confined so as not to entice males from home."

This Maryland law omitted the fact that it was intended for female dogs.

C

canines

The Associated Press reported on January 24, 2003, that Raymond Poore, Jr., called his wife at work from their Winchester, Virginia, home and told her that the dog had bitten him and he intended to kill it. When she arrived home she discovered blood and dog hair on the broken stock of a shotgun and the smell of gunpowder in the air. She then saw her unconscious husband bloodied from scratches, dog bites, and a gaping hole in his chest. Police surmised that Raymond Poore was pummeling the couple's thirty-pound shar-pei with the butt of a loaded shotgun when the weapon discharged—frightening the dog and killing poor Raymond.

According to an April 15, 1999, Reuters article, Pamela Bowers was surprised when she looked out of her kitchen window to see her border collie Brenna's doghouse flying through the air—with Brenna in it. "The flying kennel was the most incredible thing I've ever seen. I just thought 'The dog's in there,'" Bowers was quoted as saying.

A freak tornado near Sudbury, Suffolk, in eastern England, was responsible for lifting the kennel and the dog and flinging them about twenty feet across the garden. "Luckily Brenna was not seriously hurt. . . . She ran inside and hid under the sofa for an hour," Bowers said.

canines

C censorship

In order to teach government employees how to respond to Freedom of Information Act (FOIA) requests, the U.S. Department of Defense (DOD) created a video in 2004 called *The People's Right to Know*. But when the Associated Press filed a FOIA request for a copy of the $70,500 video, it took the DOD a year and a half to release it, because the Pentagon needed to censor it first. "We knew it would be embarrassing," said army lawyer Suzanne Council.

Her explanation: "We couldn't get approval" from the owners of a number of movie clips used in the video. "We did our darnedest." The FOIA grants the government permission to censor or remove sensitive information, but there is no provision for removing copyrighted material. Maybe they should change the name of the video from *The People's Right to Know* to *The People's Rights?* *No!*

President Lincoln has long been admired as a great and fair president. However, during the Civil War, Lincoln did a few things that would be considered downright un-American. In 1861, the Lincoln administration not only censored the news but also closed down publication of the *New York News* for antiadministration editorials. In 1863, they closed them down again for alleged spy activity. Lincoln liked a good joke—he could apparently dish it out but he couldn't take it. When the *New York World* satirized Lincoln in 1863 he personally ordered the paper shut down and its editors arrested. How can anyone be expected to act civil during a war, anyhow?

C chairs

The Seattle Police Department required the twenty-six employees in its fingerprint unit to attend a half-hour mandatory training session on how to sit in a chair. The safety class evolved after three employees filed workers' compensation claims for injuries they sustained after they hurt themselves attempting to sit in chairs with rollers. "Some people know how to sit in a chair," said department safety officer Patrick Sweeney, "while others need some instruction." The proper technique, according to an internal memo, is, "Take hold of the arms and get control of the chair before sitting down."

communication

An Eastlake, Ohio, high school sent out notes to the homes of all seniors informing them that they would have to "leave the state immediately after the ceremony." North High School immediately issued a correction stating: "The graduates will leave the State Theatre immediately after the ceremony," United Press International (UPI) reported on June 8, 2009. However, the correction was in need of its own correction as it told students to be at the theater no later than 3:45 a.m. instead of the intended 3:45 p.m.

C

A l Byrd of Carroll, Georgia, received a phone call from a Marietta demolition company stating that the three-bedroom house his father built had been successfully leveled. When he received the news, Byrd was demolished himself because he had never hired a company to destroy his family home. According to a June 10, 2009, *Atlanta Journal-Constitution* article, Byrd said, "It's just incredulous that something like this can happen and no one contacts the owner."

The demolition company used GPS coordinates to lead them to the house, but their intended target was most likely the abandoned building across the street. Although Byrd's house was vacant, it was filled with family heirlooms—all of which were destroyed. "My mom's dining room set, her hutch with her dishes in there," Byrd said.

In preparation for Russia Day, a patriotic holiday celebrating the country's independence after the breakup of the Soviet Union, the Russian Air Force "seeded" clouds over Moscow with a mixture of silver iodide, liquid nitrogen, and cement powder in an attempt to stimulate rain. The plan was to force the rain early so that it wouldn't rain on the day of the event. But there was a slight communications breakdown in that apparently not all the crewmembers were notified that the bags of cement had to be opened first.

A police spokesman explained in a June 17, 2008, Reuters article that "a pack of cement used in creating good weather in the capital region failed to pulverize completely at high altitude and fell on the roof of a house." The homeowner refused 50,000 rubles (US$2,100) for the two-and-a-half -to-three-foot hole in her roof, saying she'd rather "sue for damages and compensation for moral suffering."

communication

councils

During an annual convention of the National Council of Teachers of English, some members suggested eliminating the word "English" from the title of their organization because they taught not only English but also a variety of languages in school. Another group wanted to drop "National" because the word appeals to nationalism. Still another group wanted "Teachers" dropped because they wanted to be known by more politically correct terms such as "facilitator" or "guides." Apparently there were no objections to "Council of." But let's just wait until their next meeting.

clowns | C

During his 2001 campaign, the premier of Quebec, Bernard Landry, suggested the province increase spending by about US$11 million to help local graduates obtain jobs in Quebec. So what's so funny about this proposal? The money would go to clowns. Quebec's National Circus School turns out eight to ten graduates a year who are quickly snapped up by circuses around the world. According to an article in the February 13, 2001, edition of the *Montreal Gazette*, Landry wanted to increase the number of graduates to twenty-five in the hopes that more will join Quebec's own Cirque du Soleil. Of course, if the clowns can't get a job in the Cirque du Soleil, they can always get a job in government.

"'GIGGLES THE CLOWN' JAILED ON SEX CHARGES"

—ASSOCIATED PRESS HEADLINE, MAY 3, 2007

C

clowns

A judge ordered Westchester County, New York, to pay Richard Hobbs, who is a twice-convicted pedophile, a candidate for the Westchester County legislature on the Right to Life Party, and a professional clown, $2,500 for violating his rights after refusing to allow him to perform his clown act in front of children at a local amusement park.

In October 2006, Kenneth Kahn announced he was running for mayor of Alameda, California, and he wasn't just clowning around this time. Kahn, who is known professionally as "Kenny the Clown," admitted he was a long shot, not because he's a clown (almost a prerequisite these days), but because he's never run for elected office before. "People ask me, 'Do we really want to elect a clown for mayor of the city?'" Kahn said. "I say, 'That's an excellent question.'"

The answer to that question, however, was ultimately "no." Kenneth Kahn got only 7 percent of the vote, losing out to candidate Beverly Johnson. It's probably a good thing that Kahn didn't become mayor because the person who would have eventually succeeded him would have had some pretty big shoes to fill.

According to an April 23, 2009, *Daily Telegraph* article, a circus clown in Liverpool, England, was ordered not to perform while wearing his classic oversized shoes because he could trip and injure someone.

C computers

In 1947, the U.S. Navy's Mark II computer at Harvard University crashed after a moth got jammed in a relay switch. The operators removed the fried flutter-by and taped it in their logbook alongside the explanation of the occurrence.

It's a true story, but contrary to the urban legend, this isn't where the term "bug" (as in "computer bug") originated. A newspaper report from 1889, cited in the Oxford English Dictionary, related that Thomas Edison "had been up the two previous nights searching for a bug in his phonograph." And the 1934 edition of Webster's dictionary also gave the definition of bug as it related to a screwup in a mechanical or electrical devise.

Four New York City police officers, acting on an intelligence report on the location of a known suspect, went to the home of Walter and Rose Martin in Brooklyn, broke a window, and entered the residence. Police didn't find who they were looking for and apologized to Walter and Rose, who are retired and both in their eighties. But this isn't the first time the house was raided. In fact, it's been wrongly visited or raided more than fifty times since 2002 because of a computer glitch that continues to send police to their house.

According to a March 19, 2010, article in the *New York Post*, when the software was originally installed, an operator tested it by randomly typing in an address, which happened to be the Martins', and the raids began. Police assured the elderly couple that the computer problem has been fixed, but Rose said she wanted a signed letter to that effect because they had been promised that before.

"In the future computers will probably not weigh any more than 1.5 ton."
—POPULAR MECHANICS, 1949

C

computers

A dozen students sued Southern Methodist University in Texas for unspecified damages because a computer course was too hard and all twelve students in the class failed. University officials offered the twelve a chance to repeat the course, but the students insisted on getting their money back. Some students claiming to have taken time from work to attend the class sought further compensation.

On June 3, 1980, computers alerted U.S. Strategic Air Command in Omaha, Nebraska, that a Soviet submarine missile attack was in progress. One hundred B-52s were scrambled and in the air within a matter of minutes but were called off before they could launch a counterattack—which was a good thing because there was no Soviet missile attack. It wasn't a war game, either. A forty-six-cent computer chip had malfunctioned and caused the computer to nearly start World War III. Everyone at SAC breathed a sigh of relief until three days later when the same mistake happened again.

condoms

According to a March 3, 2010, article in the *Daily Telegraph*, family planning groups and the Swiss AIDS Federation have campaigned the Swiss government to approve production of an extra small condom for boys as young as twelve years old. The condom, called the Hotshot, is smaller in circumference than a "standard" condom by about five-sixteenths of an inch. The two organizations pleaded with the government following several studies that adolescent boys were not using proper protection when engaging in intercourse.

C

condoms

A twenty-three-year-old man from Madrid, Spain, was out on the town with his girlfriend and thought he was going to get lucky. He stopped by a condom machine outside a pharmacy, put in the coins, and pulled the plunger, but nothing happened. The man pounded on the machine trying to loosen the condom package, but it wouldn't budge. Noticing the spontaneity of the moment quickly slipping by, he slipped his hand into the slot and immediately got two of his fingers caught. Try as he might he couldn't get his fingers out, and he was forced to stand there for four hours, enduring humiliating comments from passersby, until help arrived and freed his fingers. It wasn't reported if the man ever got his condoms or not, but it's a sure thing that his finger was the only thing that got tugged on that night.

condoms

The District of Columbia's HIV-prevention program passed out free condoms to high school- and college-age adults but was met with some complaints—not from parents or Catholics but from the students themselves. The *Washington Post* reported on May 21, 2010, that the students complained that the condoms were substandard and that the organization should give away gold-colored packages of Trojan Magnums, giving them, said one city official, "a little bit of the bling quality."

condoms

An AIDS-awareness drive distributed thousands of government-issued safe-sex packs in South Africa that included free condoms and information about AIDS. The packs were soon recalled when it was discovered that the free condoms had been attached to the pamphlets with staples.

Lino Missio, an Italian physics student, devised a condom that plays a selection of Beethoven if it breaks during use. The inventor announced that the condom is coated with a substance that, if ruptured, will change electrical conductivity and set off a microchip to produce the music. Missio, who now owns a patent on the conductive conducting condom, said he might replace the music with a verbal warning, which, if the condom breaks during use, will warn the user to stop what he's doing. But if the condom is being used correctly—how is anyone going to hear a thing?

COWS | C

A lot of things can hit your windshield while driving, such as small rocks and bugs, but one Austrian woman really had a cow when she saw what had struck her windshield—it was a cow. According to the Austria Press Agency, in June 2002, a thirty-six-year-old woman was injured after a cow fell and landed on the hood of her car. The cow's fatal fall had occurred after it strayed from a hillside onto the flat roof of a tunnel, lost its hoofing, and plummeted just as the car emerged from the tunnel. The woman's car quickly went from cloth seats to all leather upholstery.

A law in Fruit Hill, Kentucky, demands that a man must remove his hat when coming face-to-face with a cow on any public road.

C

Professor José Antonio Visintin of the University of São Paulo in Brazil and his team attempted to clone the first cow, but the results weren't what they expected—they ended up with an ox. Visintin had two possible explanations as to what happened, according to an April 30, 2002, article on Ananova.com: Either a lab assistant had accidentally inseminated the cow with an ox embryo or, as Vinsintin said, "She must have cheated on us!"

A college student in Johnson, Vermont, became angry with her writing professor after she was given a poor grade on an essay that was required for her graduation. According to a June 7, 2001, article in the *Burlington Free Press*, she allegedly threw a pair of cow eyeballs at him. The student's essay was on the horrors of slaughterhouses.

In April 2006, a dead cow floated lazily down the West Fork River in West Virginia and became caught on a tree branch at the West Milford Dam, causing a real stink for local residents. Concerned citizens made several cattle calls to local government agencies who never kowtowed to the complaints, claiming the cow wasn't under their jurisdiction. The bloated bovine was outside city limits so it wasn't the town's responsibility; not a wild animal so not the state Department of Natural Resources' responsibility; posed no ecological danger so not the Department of Environmental Protection's problem; the state Agriculture Department called it a local issue; and a regional water board washed their hands of any responsibility. Finally, on May 13, 2006, brave workers from the state Division of Highways, along with local volunteer firefighters, removed the carcass without cowering.

COWS

C criminals

It was a synchronized robbery that still has police in Oak Ridge, Tennessee, scratching their heads. The first robber entered a local market and placed two dollars on the counter to attract the clerk's attention. The second robber, gun in hand, burst through the door and demanded money. The clerk obliged by giving the second robber the first robber's two dollars. Both robbers then beat a hasty retreat. According to a June 2009 article in the *Oak Ridger*, investigators still have no suspects in the crime.

"It is mandatory for a motorist with criminal intentions to stop at the city limits and telephone the chief of police as he is entering the town."

—TACOMA, WASHINGTON, LAW

A prisoner in Buenos Aires, who was released after serving fourteen years for murder, was arrested only seven minutes after he left prison—having gone only two hundred yards. He was charged with possession of stolen property, which he had obtained while behind bars.

A suspect in a fourteen-year-old double murder finally came forward and surrendered himself to police. Did the man's conscious finally get the better of him? Was he ready to make amends and seek forgiveness for his crimes? Nope. He wanted to collect the $3,000 reward that had been offered for his capture. The police rewarded him all right—with an all-expenses-paid trip to jail. "We believe he was serious about the reward. He will not be eligible," said Sheriff Lawrence Crow, Jr. And now he won't be eligible for anything, including parole, for a long, long time.

Thomas James and Michael Gregory Thomas of Columbia, South Carolina, planned everything about their robbery of a cell phone store except their disguises. Instead of masks the two robbers decided to spray paint their faces gold in an attempt to hide their identity. After the robbery, James began having difficulty breathing, and Thomas called for help. (Good thing they just robbed a cell phone store, right?) Before Thomas could get him to a hospital, though, James died, apparently from paint fumes or an allergic reaction. Thomas was charged with armed robbery. "It's the damnedest one I've ever had in thirty-four years," said Richland County sheriff Leon Lott. "Justice gets served in interesting ways sometimes."

STUPID

"Burglars are prohibited from entering or leaving the scene of a crime by the front door."

—LINCOLN, NEBRASKA, ORDINANCE

dead **D**

Everyone in Hartford, Connecticut, is dead! At least according to computer records. During an investigation in the mid-1980s into why Hartford's residents had been excluded from federal grand juries for three years, it was discovered that a computer error had listed everyone in town as dead. How? The city's name had been inputted into the wrong section of the records, forcing the "d" in Hartford into the column on jury information. So whenever the random jury selector chose someone from Hartford, the computer recognized the "d" in the column as "dead." Since Hartford is the insurance capital of the world, it makes you wonder how many life insurance policies were cashed in.

According to a police report, the last words of twenty-five-year-old Scott Riley were, "Shoot me, shoot me," you "ain't got the . . ." Philadelphia, Pennsylvania, television station WCAU reported that Riley had gotten into an argument with an armed twenty-four-year-old, Joseph Jimenez, over a game of beer pong.

defense

In October 1996, one day after pleading guilty to hiring a hit man, Charles S. Shapiro begged a Montgomery County, Maryland, court to allow him to change his plea. He claimed his judgment had been impaired because he had ingested tranquilizers along with an entire bottle of extra-strength Tums before he confessed.

Bruce Tuck of Martin, Tennessee, confessed to a series of rapes, according to a June 19, 2010, article in the *Knoxville News Sentinel*. Tuck, who was sentenced to sixty years and faces additional charges, went back to court to have his case thrown out because he was not of sound mind when he made his confession. The 275-pound Tuck claimed that the jail had him on a "lettuce-only" diet before his trial and when a detective offered him a bag of chips to admit the charge, he confessed.

Troy Matthew Gentzler confessed to tossing rocks at cars from an overpass on Interstate 83 near York, Pennsylvania. His lawyer claimed he was the victim of "roid rage," erratic emotional swings caused by steroid use.

In Dodge City, Kansas, on April 16, 1991, five drunk and stoned teenagers randomly attacked and shot a twenty-six-year-old stranger, killing him on the spot. The teenagers' defense attorneys claimed their clients had been hypnotized by the Houston-based rap group the Geto Boys. (Note: This is the first case to use music-induced insanity as a defense in a murder trial.)

D

The origin of the "Twinkie defense": On November 27, 1978, Dan White, a former police officer and a member of San Francisco's board of supervisors, shot to death the city's mayor, George Moscone, and Harvey Milk, the board's first openly gay supervisor. White's attorneys brought in a team of psychiatrists who each attempted to explain why White had murdered the two men. One psychiatrist delved into White's junk-food addiction, especially to Twinkies, Coca-Cola, and potato chips. He explained that because of all the junk food White had consumed, his blood-sugar levels might have compounded his manic depression and contributed to the killings. On May 21, 1979, White was convicted of involuntary manslaughter. He later committed suicide.

A potential legal defense is being considered by a group of professionals who failed to file their income tax returns on time. They claim they suffer from an anxiety syndrome characterized by "an overall inability to act in [their] own interest." According to a psychiatry professor, victims are "highly ambitious, hypercritical, detail-oriented people," who cannot relax, don't trust others to do work assigned to them, and have a tendency to procrastinate and become secretive.

"Black rage" was the defense used by Colin Ferguson, who is black, to explain why he killed four whites and two Asian Americans on a Long Island Railroad train. This syndrome is a type of insanity caused by exposure to prolonged racial prejudice in the United States. Ferguson is Jamaican.

The lawyer for Daimion Osby, a black eighteen-year-old who shot two unarmed blacks in a Fort Worth parking lot in 1993, deadlocked the jury after he argued that Osby suffered from "urban survival syndrome"—a fear that inner-city residents have of other people in their same area.

déjà vu

Thirty-nine-year-old Gerald Maxwell was caught and arrested in 2009 for breaking into a Sarasota, Florida, home. According to an August 4, 2010, report on television station WWSB, Maxwell was caught breaking into the exact same residence again but quickly tried to explain his innocence by telling the arresting officers, "I was going back in there to leave a thank-you note, because I'm the guy who burglarized this place last year [and] I just got out of jail."

"It's déjà vu all over again": Yogi Berra, American Major League Baseball player and manager, explained that this quote originated after he witnessed Yankees Mickey Mantle and Roger Maris hit back-to-back home runs in the early 1960s.

"If at first you don't succeed, try, try again,"
must have been running through the mind of
this story's repeat offender sometime during his
short criminal career. The Troy, Alabama, man
was arrested and pled guilty to breaking into
the Deja Vu store—twice. Our recidivist, who
apparently wasn't very original, smashed the same
window and stole much of the same merchandise.
He was arrested because the same witness
identified him both times. I wonder if he'll get off
because of the rule of double jeopardy?

dentists

Neville Kan, a dentist in Chiswick, England, was acquitted of professional misconduct after being accused of drilling a hole in a patient's tooth and refusing to fill it until the patient paid the £35 she still owed. According to a July 18, 2003, *Daily Telegraph* report, the victim, identified as Mrs. B, claimed Kan told her, "Nothing lasts forever, I am not going to last forever. . . . Nothing in life is free. You owe me money." Even if the dentist was acquitted he'll never receive a plaque for that kind of behavior.

diagnoses | D

The following are actual diagnostic notations given by doctors.

 "The patient is married but sexually active."

 "She does indeed have a fear of frying and mental problems that she attributes to deep-fat fryers."

 "The patient's father died at age sixty-five, but he has not been seen for some time."

 "The patient has crap in his cast with walking [instead of 'cramps in his calves']".

 "When standing with eyes closed, he missed his right finger to his nose and has to search for it on the left side."

 "The patient is a fifty-three-year-old police officer who was found unconscious by his bicycle."

 "Her father died from a heart attack at age twelve."

D | discipline

The preferred "disciplinary" method of Olayinka Alege, the assistant principal of King High School in Tampa, Florida, is toe popping. Alege orders unruly students to remove their shoes so he can "pop" their toes, according to a July 24, 2009, article in the *Tampa Tribune*. A group of five students filed a complaint against Alege indicating that although the "popping" doesn't hurt, it is a little "weird." One recidivist student allegedly has had his toes popped twenty times. The Tampa sheriff's office investigated how Alege makes his students toe the line but the digital disciplinarian was cleared of all charges.

A ccording to a September 26, 2002, article in the *Houston Chronicle*, the stepfather of an eight-year-old boy admitted to a very shocking form of disciple. Child-welfare officials removed the boy from the house after the man brazenly admitted using a stun gun on the child as punishment for being late for school.

I n March 2000 a judge in Dedham, Massachusetts, sentenced Thomas Flanagan to nine years in prison for the nearly continuous physical abuse of his wife and three children. Flanagan was indicted on three counts of attempted murder and thirty-nine counts of assault and battery, including what the children referred to as "plucking." The kids told investigators working on Flanagan's case that their father made them line up every day for "plucking," in which he would take a pair of tweezers and pluck out their nose hair—making Flanagan the winner of the "plucking" worst father of the year award.

D

discipline

According to the Associated Press, on July 10, 2009, seventy-three-year-old H. Beatty Chadwick was finally released from a Pennsylvania jail after serving more than fourteen years behind bars. Chadwick was the longest-serving prisoner to be incarcerated without ever having been charged with a crime. During divorce proceedings in 1995, a judge had ordered Chadwick to jail until such time as he turned over $2.5 million that he was accused of hiding from his ex-wife and which Chadwick always denied. Delaware County judge Joseph Cronin finally determined that continuing Chadwick's incarceration would not result in his surrendering the money.

divorce | D

A man in Tariffville, Connecticut, filed for divorce because his wife left him a note on the refrigerator that read: "I won't be home when you return from work. Have gone to the bridge club. There'll be a recipe for your dinner at 7 o'clock on Channel 2."

A man in Hazard, Kentucky, divorced his wife because she "beat him whenever he removed onions from his hamburger without first asking for permission."

The South Dakota Supreme Court upheld a divorce court ruling in September 1994, citing the husband as the cause of the couple's troubles. He had, among other bad habits, a tendency of passing gas around the house and getting angry with his wife when she complained. The wife claimed her husband could easily regulate his odoriferous emissions and would break wind as a "retaliation thing."

D

During a 1990 divorce case, Judge Paul Marko of Broward County, Florida, told Marianne Price that he forbade her from having male suitors visit her or stay the night in her house because it was formerly joint property. The judge further stated that since Price's husband was now staying in his "own" apartment he could have the "entire [Miami] Dolphins cheerleading squad running though his apartment naked." Judge Marko then suggested to Price that she start frequenting singles bars: "I've been [in singles bars]. I'm a single man. There are all kinds of . . . guys running around in open shirts with eagles on their chests. There are great guys out there." He then explained to Price that if she was caught having a live-in lover, he would order her house to be sold, saying, "I don't want her all of a sudden taking up with some nice, sweet, little blond from Norway."

Later Judge Marko expressed his most sincere apologies to Price. Months later, his decision was overturned by a higher court.

Walter Kern of Long Island filed for divorce against his wife, Rana, claiming that she is a witch and routinely practices ritualistic animal sacrifices.

A deaf man in Bennettsville, South Carolina, filed for divorce because his wife "was always nagging him in sign language."

A woman in Canon City, Colorado, divorced her husband because he forced her to "duck under the dashboard whenever they drove past his girlfriend's house."

A woman in Hardwick, Georgia, divorced her husband on the grounds that he "stayed home too much and was much too affectionate."

D

divorce

A man in Smelterville, Idaho, filed for divorce because, his claim stated, "His wife dressed up as a ghost and tried to scare his elderly mother out of the house."

A man in Honolulu, Hawaii, asked for divorce because his wife "served pea soup for breakfast and dinner . . . and packed his lunch with pea sandwiches."

A man in Winthrop, Maine, divorced his wife because she "wore earplugs whenever his mother came to visit."

A woman in Frackville, Pennsylvania, filed for divorce citing the fact that her husband insisted on "shooting tin cans off her head with a slingshot."

dna

"**F**or almost 20 years," wrote a *Boston Globe* reporter in a March 24, 2002, article, "convicted rapist Benjamin LaGuer (incarcerated at the Massachusetts Correctional Institution at Norfolk) has waged a public campaign maintaining his innocence." LaGuer was serving time for the sexual attack of an elderly woman but had a group of supporters who believed in his innocence. Those supporters raised $30,000 for a DNA test in hopes of once and for all proving that LaGuer didn't perpetrate the crime. On March 22, 2002, the DNA test conclusively proved that the sperm found on the victim was LaGuer's.

C'est la guerre!

D

dna

Forty-six-year-old David Holland submitted to police in San Jose, California, and gave a DNA sample in order to prove his innocence in the murder investigation of his brother. According to a November 20, 2007, article in the *San Francisco Chronicle*, he was then arrested for a previously unsolved 2001 rape when his DNA sample matched sperm left behind by the rapist.

Lawyer Steven Wise, promoting his book *Drawing the Line: Science and the Case for Animal Rights*, at a Washington, D.C., bookstore, told audience members that because some animals experience emotions, use language, and interact socially, "I don't see a difference between a chimpanzee and my four-and-a-half-year-old son" based on the fact that "chimps have 98 percent of DNA in common with humans." The *Toronto Star* reported on June 15, 2002, that Wise's son, Christopher, was not in the audience and was therefore unavailable for comment.

An article in the *Journal of Agricultural and Food Chemistry*, and reported in the January 19, 2005, issue of *New Scientist*, showed that rates of DNA-damaging cancers caused by heterocyclic amines, a carcinogen found in cooked meat, were lower in rats that drank water than in rats that drank nonalcoholic beer.

Marshall Thomas, who was charged in 1999 with rape in Belleville, Illinois, demanded and received a DNA test he knew would make the prosecutor drop all charges. According to a February 15, 2002, article in the *Belleville News Democrat*, the results of the DNA test matched an earlier, unsolved rape, and the 1999 rape case is still pending.

D doctors

Some doctors lack appropriate bedside manner but one nationally recognized La Jolla, California, cardiologist beat everyone else to the punch. Dr. Maurice Buchbinder was accused of making "chopping-like blows to the patient's abdomen," trying to hit his leg "with a substantial amount of force," and using "the tip of his elbow to hit [him] on the forehead," the *San Diego Union-Tribune* reported on September 26, 2007. The patient was placed on a gurney following angioplasty and was attacked by Buchbinder, who yelled, "You are an animal" and then "grabbed and twisted the patient's nose," making it turn "bluish," witnesses told reporters. Scripps Memorial Hospital placed Buchbinder on indefinite suspension while it launched its own investigation.

doughnuts

"**Y**ou Have the Right to Remain Glazed," is emblazoned on caps and T-shirts available from the Cops and Doughnuts shop, the former Clare City Bakery in Clare, Michigan. The store, which had been around for 113 years, was purchased by the Clare Police Department, according to a July 3, 2009, report on WNEM-TV in Saginaw. The officers will not be paid for their services and the shop will be staffed by high school and college students. Please insert your joke here: _____.

It is illegal in Oak Park, Illinois, to cook more than one hundred doughnuts in a single day.

D

doughnuts

After receiving a free Krispy Kreme doughnut at a store promotion in Erie, Pennsylvania, a seventeen-year-old boy jumped back in line and asked for another doughnut but was refused. The boy returned moments later with a McDonald's bag over his head, according to the August 25, 2003, edition of the *Erie Times-News*, and demanded another doughnut but was thwarted again. After this second rejection the boy fell to the floor and began thrashing his arms and legs about, screaming for another doughnut. He was cited for disorderly conduct.

Houston, Texas, ambulance driver Larry A. Wesley was suspended in July 2000 because, while transporting an injured child to the Ben Taub General Hospital, he stopped to get doughnuts and juice. Wesley filed an unlawful discrimination lawsuit, claiming intentional infliction of emotional distress and stating that had he been a white man he wouldn't have been disciplined so seriously. According to a July 13, 2007, article in the *Houston Chronicle*, a federal judge awarded Wesley a big doughnut by throwing his case out of court. The doughnut-eating EMS driver was left with a glazed look in his eyes.

drugs

D

A woman called the police and was incensed because she believed someone had ripped her off. When police questioned her about the substandard merchandise, she told them it was two rocks. Was she talking about diamonds? Nope. She was talking about two rocks of crack cocaine. A police officer was dispatched to the woman's residence where the woman angrily showed the fifty-dollar rocks of cocaine and complained they tasted like baking soda. The officer ran a field test on the rocks, they registered as real cocaine, and he arrested the incensed (or senseless) woman on the spot.

"It's amazing," said assistant police chief Jerry Potts. "We've had people call and try to report robberies over dope, but we've never had someone call and say they got ripped off on a dope deal, and then we checked the cocaine and it actually was cocaine."

D

drugs

Robert Cisero of Medford, Oregon, was arrested, according to a June 12, 2008, Associated Press article, after he allegedly used a hammer to hit his teenage daughter in the ankle. Police reported that Cisero bludgeoned his daughter to feign a "skating" injury so she could obtain painkillers, which he then stole from her and took.

In March 1993, Jane Bryne, then forty-two, was arrested in Clayton, Missouri, on drug-possession charges. She was in the second row of a courtroom at the time, observing the trial of her boyfriend, up on robbery charges, when her purse slipped from her grasp and fell to the floor. A chivalrous police officer who was sitting in the row in front of Bryne helped her pick up the contents and noticed, among the small cosmetic bottles, a vial filled with cocaine.

A n article from the April 14, 2005, issue of the *Barre-Montpelier Times Argus* told the story of seventeen-year-old Nickolas Buckalew of Morrisville, Vermont, who was charged with digging up a corpse. After Buckalew dug up the dead body on April 8, he hacked off the head and took it with him (it was later found near his home). Court documents report that Buckalew had bragged about stealing the head and told people that his intention was to make a bong out of it. On June 28, 2006, he was sentenced to one to seven years for the mutilation of the corpse. Had Buckalew succeeded in making the bong, it would have been an actual "pot head."

D

ducks

In the city of Stark, Kansas, it is
against the law to quack like a duck.

Professor Trevor Cox from the University
of Salford in England, his team of fellow
acoustic researchers, and a duck named Daisy
debunked once and for all the myth that a
duck's quack doesn't have an echo. The *Guardian*
reported on Cox's acoustic experiments with
Daisy in a September 8, 2003, article in which
the professor stated the reason the myth started
could be that "a duck quacks rather quietly, so
the sound coming back is at a low level and
might not be heard." Cox explained ducks are
also normally found in open-water areas and are
seldom found quacking around echoic cliffs.

"STUFFED DUCK EXPLOSION ENDS BADLY"

—*NEWTON (MA) TAB* HEADLINE, MARCH 5, 2005

A s reported in a May 20, 2009, article in the *Guardian*, two scientists from Britain's University of Oxford spent three years and nearly $500,000 to discover that ducks, who are known to love swimming in ponds, might be even more comfortable standing under a sprinkler. The study, said lead researcher Marian Stamp Dawkins, concluded that ducks basically just like water.

"BRITISH DUCKS HAVE REGIONAL ACCENTS, RESEARCHERS SAY"

—BBC News headline, June 4, 2004

excuses

A library employee from Portland State University in Oregon admitted that she had stolen more than $200,000 over the years from the school's copy machines. According to the school's newspaper, the *Vanguard*, the woman begged for mercy citing, in her defense, that she was just temporarily using the money anyway. The woman claimed that she had spent almost the entire amount on government-sponsored video poker machines, and since she never won more than she put in, the state eventually got all its money back.

"I will be in space that day."

THIS EXCUSE WAS GIVEN BY A REAL ASTRONAUT IN HARRIS COUNTY DISTRICT COURT IN HOUSTON, TEXAS, AFTER HE RECEIVED A JURY DUTY LETTER. THE ASTRONAUT WAS RESCHEDULED AND ASKED TO RETURN AFTER SPLASHDOWN.

In January 1995, Pamela Baker asked a Beaufort, South Carolina, judge to excuse her from jury duty in a murder trial. She claimed her husband, Baptist pastor Karl Baker, forbade her from speaking in public.

In May 1996, Jenny Lee Owens, thirty-nine, explained to a London, Ohio, court why her boyfriend was shot to death: "Something came into the room. It was not a person. It was like a color. Me and it, whatever it was, we both had the gun. Somehow it had passed into me. It was holding the gun; I was standing behind it." Together Jenny Lee Owens and "it" walked down the hall, "it" aimed the gun, and "it" shot Jenny's boyfriend in the back of the head. Too bad "it" never showed up in court.

"I can't keep a secret."

—AN EXCUSE GIVEN TO JUDGE B. MICHAEL DANN OF ARIZONA BY A BLABBERMOUTH TRYING TO AVOID JURY DUTY

Januice Brown was found guilty by a Texas jury in the shooting death of her husband. Brown's defense was that she killed her husband to prevent aliens from torturing him forever.

excuses

E

Timothy Pereira was driving 85 mph in a 35 mph zone down a road in Salem, Massachusetts, swerved into oncoming traffic, and crashed head-on into Christine Speliotis's car. The accident was obviously Pereira's fault. But according to an August 1, 2009, article in the *Salem News*, Brandon Pereira, the seventeen-year-old cousin of Timothy, sued Speliotis, claiming that had her reflexes been quicker she could have gotten out of the way and the accident would never have occurred.

According to an August 12, 2009, report from the Canadian Broadcasting Corporation News, authorities in Deer Lake, Newfoundland, decided not to press charges against three boys whom they suspected of harassing a young moose so severely it had to be put down. The prosecuting attorney informed the court of its decision after they received an alibi from one of the boys' fathers. The man claimed that the three boys couldn't be responsible for the moose harassment because, at the time, they were busy vandalizing a nearby church.

explanations

A twenty-two-year-old man was arrested while being chased by an angry mob of people in Kitsap, Washington. According to an August 12, 2009, article in the *Kitsap Sun*, the man admitted he had tossed rocks at the people but explained that he was preparing to become an Ultimate Fighting Championship fighter. The man told arresting officers that he had never actually been in a fight before and wanted to know how it felt to get beaten up.

Known mobster Vincent "Gigi Portalla" Marino has complained for years that federal agents planted something on him during surgery to remove a bullet from his buttocks. Marino was granted a hearing to reveal the truth, and the region's top federal law enforcement official denied his claim that federal agents had put a tracking device in his butt.

"We can confirm that the U.S. Drug Enforcement Administration did not implant a tracking device in defendant Vincent M. 'Gigi Portalla' Marino's buttocks," U.S. attorney Donald Stern said in a statement. "But we cannot speak, however, for any extraterrestrial beings." U.S. district judge Nathaniel Gorton said the situation "sounds like some DEA agent trying to be funny," but he honored Marino's request to force the government to tell him the truth about the device.

Maybe that's where the expression "having a bug up your butt" came from.

"I do touch too much bread, yes, more than the next person."

—Samuel Feldman, convicted of fondling $1,000 worth of baked goods in Philadelphia stores

A man who had just robbed a U.S. Bank branch in Sacramento, California, explained his actions to a bank employee: "I only wanted to teach you a lesson. I want a job in bank security." The man's claims would have had more merit had he not been previously convicted of five bank robberies with another bank robbery conviction pending.

A n officer approached the driver of a car he had pulled over for speeding, and the man gave a very convincing excuse: "My wife is ovulating," he told the officer. "I have to get home right now."

R oger Hunt claimed he and his girlfriend were simply going out on a New Year's Eve dinner date in his truck when he was arrested by police. According to a January 3, 2002, article in the *Warren (OH) Tribune-Chronicle*, Hunt was charged with kidnapping when police noticed the girlfriend was barefoot, to which Hunt nervously explained, "She's from Virginia. She doesn't wear shoes [when she goes out to dinner]."

E
explanations

E | explosives

For reasons unknown, Kaleb E. Spangler duct-taped a large "mortar-style" explosive onto a football helmet, placed it on his head, got into a car with some friends, and then lit the fuse. According to an August 16, 2006, story in the *Bloomington (IN) Herald-Times*, Spangler was injured in the massive explosion. Believe it or not, alcohol was reportedly involved.

According to the *Die Krone* newspaper, in June 2003 an Austrian man walked up to his Ford Cougar, pulled out his keys, pushed the keyless entry remote, and watched as his car exploded. Police in Sollenau originally investigated the event as a possible bomb attack but soon discovered the cause was the owner's own actions. Apparently the man had two cylinders filled with oxyacetylene gas in his trunk and the values on both were slightly open. When he pushed the remote, a spark set off the gas and his Detroit steel became scrap metal.

Australians Ricki Stanley and Damian Jackson were working on Stanley's Ute automobile when they accidentally ruptured a propane tank and couldn't shut off the gas. Instead of trying to seal the leak, the two Hallam, Victoria, men decided to go inside for a small coffee. While they were waiting for the kettle to boil, gas filled the basement, and before the kettle whistled the house exploded. The house was lifted a full six inches off its foundation, according to the June 6, 2005, article in the *Melbourne Herald Sun*, and sustained nearly $400,000 in damages. Stanley had a warning to other would-be home mechanics about using propane gas: "I'm never touching it again. It's taken everything away."

Well, it didn't exactly take everything away, or Stanley and his friend wouldn't be around to tell the tale.

explosives

Jerry Stromyer of Wheeling, West Virginia, was dying to be the life of the party and almost got his wish—the dying part, that is. A partygoer had tried unsuccessfully to make a blasting cap explode when Stromyer took center stage, getting everyone's attention with the famous line "Hey, watch this!" Stromyer placed the blasting cap in his mouth and bit down firmly. The March 18, 1986, explosion blew off his lips, teeth, and tongue. I'm sure one smart-ass in the crowd said, "That Stromyer, he's always shooting off his mouth."

family F

An Oregon, Wisconsin, man was arrested, according to a February 13, 2009, article in the *Wisconsin State Journal*, after his nine-year-old son's teacher turned over to the principal a story written by the young boy in which he tells about the time his father shot him in the buttocks with a BB gun because he was standing in front of the television.

STUPID

"No person shall knowingly keep or harbor at his house or her house within the city any woman of ill-repute, lewd character, or a common prostitute . . . other than wife, mother, or sister."

—ASHLAND, KENTUCKY, ORDINANCE

F

The father of a nineteen-year-old was arrested in Baltimore, according to a February 24, 2009, Associated Press article, because his son refused to remove his hat during church service.

Television station KVVU-TV in Las Vegas reported on January 1, 2009, that Robert Blue had been arrested and charged with chaining his fifteen-year-old daughter to her bed at night to keep her from eating. Blue explained his actions to police by stating that he wanted his daughter, who weighs 165 pounds, to lose 20 pounds, which would put her at her ideal fighting weight for mixed martial arts.

According to a January 5, 2009, CNN piece, Doug and Valerie Herrman reported their son missing and pleaded with the El Dorado, Kansas, sheriff's department for their assistance in helping them locate their son. The Herrmans' attorney claimed his clients were "very worried" about their son, Adam, and were finally begging the public to help them find him—even though the boy had run away ten years ago when he was eleven.

Walt and Kathy Viggiano of Wichita, Kansas, had their four children removed in 1998 because of the unsanitary condition of their mobile home. A year later, Judge James Burgess agreed to return the children to their parents because, unlike most other such cases, the Viggianos neither abused drugs or alcohol and were kind and loving to their children. According to a July 11, 1999, article in the *Wichita Eagle*, the initial investigators remarked that even though the family spoke kindly to one another they communicated entirely in Klingon from *Star Trek*.

The father of a two- and four-year-old was cited for disorderly conduct in Fond du Lac, Wisconsin, after being spotted buying beer for his children. He was cited for disorderly conduct because under Wisconsin law parents are exempt from the prohibition of providing alcohol to minors and, according to a September 24, 2008, article in *Appleton (WI) Post Crescent*, he had sworn at police.

F

family

The father of David Norris left home when his son was five months old and the two never saw each other. According to an August 26, 2008, article in the *Scottish Daily Record*, when David turned twenty-two he was sentenced to a minimum twelve-year sentence for killing a man following an earlier conviction for rape. He began serving his sentence in Peterhead prison, where he ran into thirty-nine-year-old David Gilles, who was serving a life sentence for the kidnapping and sexual torture of a young woman. You guessed it: Gilles is Norris's father.

Sheila and Paul Garcia of Northfleet, Gravesend, in England, admitted to London's *Daily Mail* on February 27, 2008, that they had allowed a thirty-six-year-old divorced man to move in with them as he was their sixteen-year-old daughter's boyfriend. Even though the Garcias admitted they didn't like the arrangement, they thought it preferable to the alternative of their daughter running away with the divorced father of one.

According to a March 6, 2008, report on CFNews13.com, authorities in Orlando, Florida, were on the lookout for two women who were caught on a surveillance camera at the Magical Car Wash. The two women were videotaped depositing coins in the car wash and then scolding and subsequently pressure-washing a small child.

Twenty-seven-year-old Aron Pritchard of Hutchinson, Kansas, was convicted of child endangerment, according to a March 10, 2008, report on Wichita's KWCH-TV. Pritchard was accused of putting his girlfriend's children, age two and three, into a hot clothes dryer and explaining to them that they could have fun without necessarily spending a lot of money.

felines

Christopher Campbell from Cedar Crest, New Mexico, was arrested and charged with cruelty to animals for the mutilation of his house cats. According to a November 8, 2002, report from KRQE-TV in Albuquerque, Campbell claimed the animals were actually supernatural entities that had merely taken the shape of friendly felines.

Cats are forbidden to ride on public buses in Seattle if there is a dog already on board. Also, any dog weighing more than twenty-five pounds must pay the full adult fare.

A researcher writing in the January–February 2007 issue of *Australasian Science* magazine reported that the protozoan *Toxoplasma gondii*, whose primary host is the domestic house cat, does more than harm the fetuses of pregnant women. Their report also concluded that toxoplasmosis could lower the IQ in men and make women more promiscuous.

feuds

Two families in the Kings Creek area north of Lenoir, North Carolina, started a reoccurring feud after a dog killed a neighbor's cat. According to sheriff's deputies, the family who owned the cat shot their neighbor's dog to death. When the family of the slain dog found out, they shot the cat's owner and the man's young daughter. As reported by Time Warner Cable's News 14 on June 28, 2009, deputies were dispatched, and the dog owner shot at them. He was fatally wounded in the ensuing gun battle.

A twenty-four-year-old Cedar City, Utah, man was given a citation for littering according to a September 10, 2002, article in the *Salt Lake Tribune*, after he allegedly shaved his head and flung the hair clippings over a fence into his neighbor's yard.

F

feuds

Two men from Virginia who had been employed by a moving company were detained by police for public intoxication in a Middlesex Township, Pennsylvania, motel parking lot. The *Harrisburg Patriot-News* reported on August 11, 2007, that the two were feuding over whether Virginia is north or south of Pennsylvania.

According to a July 10, 2008, article in London's *Daily Telegraph*, police in Crawley, West Sussex, were called to a supermarket to break up a fight between two grandmothers who were smashing into each other with their mobility scooters.

On October 14, 2009, Poland's Polskie Radio reported that a settlement had been reached in the year-and-a-half-long legal battle between two neighbors in Mikowice. The feud started when one neighbor sued the other, alleging that his neighbor had ruined his plastic bucket (valued at $4.50) by kicking it. The accused neighbor offered proof of his innocence by supplying the court with a video showing the plaintiff using the bucket after the alleged incident. But the neighbor countered the evidence by calling an "expert" witness who examined the bucket and verified that it was probably damaged.

Louis Dethy, a retired Belgian engineer, was embroiled in a feud with his ex-wife and their fourteen children. Dethy rigged nineteen deadly booby traps throughout his home near Charleroi in order to hurt anyone who attempted to take ownership of the house. According to a November 11, 2002, article in the Canada's *National Post*, Dethy must have forgotten the location of one of the traps because he was killed when he accidentally set it off.

fireworks

The *Los Angeles Times* reported on February 24, 2003, that thirty-three-year-old Luis Chavez was arrested at his Cypress, California, condominium after he, for reasons unknown, deliberately set off aerial fireworks in his bedroom—resulting in $135,000 in damages. Two years later, for reasons known (he had consumed ten beers in rapid succession), thirty-eight-year-old Steven Glenn of Plainfield, Illinois, set off a ten-inch commercial fireworks shell in the living room of a house he was renting.

"The whole house is pretty much, from the concussion of the explosion and the fire and the smoke, totaled," said Plainfield fire chief John Eichelberger. According to the May 3, 2005, report from WMAQ-TV, Chicago, Glenn was treated and released but his girlfriend, Shauna Adams, required hospitalization.

fireworks

As reported in the May 8, 2007, edition of the *Chicago Tribune*, in a cliché come to life, a twenty-nine-year-old man from Downers Grove, Illinois, decided to set off some fireworks in his yard (although it wasn't anywhere near the Fourth of July). When one of the rocket tubes didn't go off he picked it up and looked into one end to see what was wrong. Needless to say he went out with a bang.

F | flatulence

People think flatulence is gross, inappropriate, or funny, but scientists from the Australian Antarctic Division think it's awesome. As part of their research mission to track the habits of whales, the team was busy tagging the enormous mammals with satellite-tracking devices when something never before captured occurred—the whale farted. According to a September 14, 2003, article in the *Australian*, the team believes they have the first-ever photo of the water pattern made by a whale passing wind. And according to researchers, they got more than just an eyeful— they got a nose full, too. "We got away from the bow of the ship very quickly," said Nick Gales. "It does stink."

According to a March 22, 2007, story in the Scottish newspaper *Dunfermline Press*, Stewart Laidlaw, thirty-five, was banished from Thirsty Kirsty's pub in the Royal Burgh of Dunfermline, in the town of Fife, Scotland, after several customers complained about his noxious emissions. A stunned Laidlaw said no one had complained about his flatulence before but did state that a new law could be to blame. On March 26, 2006, Scotland enacted one of the toughest smoking bans in Europe and now, Laidlaw conceded, there's no smoke to cover up the smell.

It is widely understood that methane gas is a prime contributor to corrupting the ozone layer and causing the dreaded global warming—and an enormous amount of methane is created by cattle and sheep flatulence. Scientists at the Department of Primary Industries and Fisheries in Queensland, Australia, as reported in a May 3, 2002, AP article, will test forty potentially methane-reducing bacteria found in the digestive tracts of kangaroos because, for reasons yet unknown, kangaroos are less flatulent than other animals.

F

flatulence

Police thought the Canadian driver of an armored truck in Edmonton, Alberta, was trying to signal them for help by repeatedly opening and closing the truck's door. Calling for backup, the original officer and five other patrol cars pulled the armored car over to find out the true nature of the problem. It turned out there wasn't an emergency; the driver was simply trying to fan fresh air into the cab after his partner had passed gas.

> "If you don't get those cameras out of my face, I'm gonna go 8.6 on the Richter scale with gastric emissions that'll clear this room!"
>
> —CONGRESSMAN JAMES TRAFICANT (D-OH),
> TO PHOTOJOURNALISTS COVERING HIS HOUSE ETHICS
> SUBCOMMITTEE HEARING, JULY 2002

football

The Norfolk, Virginia, Blues were a team of collegiate all-stars and were considered by many, including themselves, to be the final word in college football. So when they went up against Washington D.C.'s Gallaudet University, they thought they had a sure thing: Gallaudet was a school for the hearing impaired. Norfolk's egos were bigger than their helmets, and they decided since their opponents were deaf they wouldn't even bother using signals or even to huddle. This classic 1912 blunder ended in a shutout, 20 to 0—in favor of Gallaudet. Although team members were deaf, they could still read lips and they understood every play Norfolk was going to make.

I'm sure after the game that Norfolk's fans gave their team a few signs anyone could understand.

football

"It shall be unlawful for any visiting football team or player to carry, convey, tote, kick, throw, pass, or otherwise transport or propel any inflated pigskin across the University of Arizona goal line or score a safety within the confines of the city of Tucson, County of Pima, State of Arizona."

—A TUCSON, ARIZONA, STATUTE. VIOLATORS CAN BE FINED $300 AND SENTENCED TO NOT LESS THAN THREE MONTHS IN THE CITY JAIL.

"He signed with us just to get [an engineering] education, and that's the wrong reason. I wish he had told us that [sooner]."

—UNIVERSITY OF ARKANSAS FOOTBALL COACH COMMENTING ON A DECISION BY A FRESHMAN TO FORFEIT HIS FOOTBALL SCHOLARSHIP AND RETURN HOME

fudge

The *Washington Post* reported on August 3, 2007, the arrest of Catherine Delgado, who was discovered around midnight in a hotel lobby covered in fudge with "large slabs of fudge bulging out of her pockets." Police discovered that the door of a nearby store, the Fudge Kitchen, was open and a large quantity of fudge in the window display was missing. Police confirmed that alcohol was involved.

G | gambling

Toshi Van Blitter of El Macero, California, played blackjack at two Harrah's casinos in Las Vegas and racked up $350,000 in debt. Since she hadn't done well at cards, she tried her hand at another suit—a lawsuit. In 1985, Blitter filed to have her debts canceled, claiming that Harrah's was negligent. For what? Blitter claimed Harrah's should have told her that she was an incompetent blackjack player or informed her that she should take classes on how to play the game. Her case went bust, however, when two federal judges dismissed her claim.

gambling

A man who should be spending his time in Gamblers Anonymous instead of the courtroom countersued the Sands Casino Hotel in Atlantic City in retaliation for their suit against him. The casino sued the man in an attempt to recover the more than $1 million in credit they had extended him so he could continue gambling at their casino. In turn, the gambler sued the hotel to have his debt canceled and to have the casino pay all legal expenses as well as punitive damages for the way the casino treated him. The man claimed the casino treated him very well; he was personally escorted to his gaming tables and brought complimentary drinks by a waitress who waited on him exclusively. He complained that such wonderful treatment caused him to drink too much, which inevitably led to the great monetary losses that he claimed he would have easily avoided otherwise. Yeah, I bet!

gangs

Steven Gilmore, Jr., confessed to police that he is an aspiring rap singer and felt it was imperative for him to commit a violent crime in order to gain "street cred" among his peers. Gilmore was arrested in Gainesville, Florida, according to a May 11, 2009, article in the *Gainesville Sun*, after he shot a convenience store clerk—with a BB gun.

The Harrison County School Board in Mississippi banned a Jewish student from wearing a Star of David because it was feared that it might be mistaken for a gang symbol.

A lex Fowler, who had the words "Crip for Life" tattooed on his neck, was arrested and charged with attempted robbery of a home in Jasper, Texas. According to a July 20, 2009, article in the *Beaumont Enterprise*, Fowler was thwarted in his attempt to rob the home of an eighty-seven-year-old woman after she chased him from the house threatening to spray him with a can of Raid insect repellant.

T he *New York Daily News* reported on October 11, 2009, that New York City, which is sued more than one thousand times a year, has an unwritten policy of settling some lawsuits quickly to avoid the risk of prolonged and expensive trials or excessive financial judgments. More than twenty of those lawsuits, some dating back several years, were filed by members of the East 21st Street Crew (a notorious Brooklyn-based gang known for selling crack cocaine), and the city has settled with them every time. The "civil rights" lawsuits against the city were over various criminal charges and possibly illegal searches; to date, the city has paid the gang more than $500,000.

G

gangs

Reacting to school vandalism and a downtown shooting, officials at Round Rock High School in Texas banned the color red on Friday. Apparently the gang responsible for these incidents wore red. About forty students wearing red items were sequestered in the library and their parents called. The American Civil Liberties Union remarked that it was the first known case of a school reacting to gang fears by banning a complete primary color.

On August 31, 2009, the *Minneapolis Star Tribune* reported on thirty-year-old Kenny Jackson, who was arrested in St. Paul, Minnesota, after going on a rampage in his own house, destroying furniture, and harassing his four-year-old son. Jackson, who is a member of the Bloods gang, became enraged when he saw his young son wearing a blue shirt, which happens to be the color of a rival gang.

Police in Commerce City, Colorado, were dispatched to a domestic disturbance call and arrested nineteen-year-old Joseph Manzanares, who had been fighting with his girlfriend. According to an April 10, 2008, article in the *Rocky Mountain News*, Manzanares and his girlfriend, who were in rival gangs, got into an altercation about which local street gang's colors their toddler should wear.

G | goats

Alysia Krafel of Red Bluff, California, arrived home to find her 215-pound goat King George stuck in an oak tree hanging from a hoof. Krafel supposed that King George had climbed the tree to eat leaves and got himself lodged in the branches. "I sprayed Pam all over everything to try and grease it," she said, but that didn't help him get free. A neighbor heard Krafel's call and King George's bleats for help and came over and cut the tree down to free the goat. A reporter for the *Red Bluff Daily News* asked Krafel if she thought her goat had learned a lesson, to which she responded, no, "He's a goat."

In Massachusetts it is illegal
for a goat to wear trousers.

A man from the southern Nigerian village of Isseluku was arrested for murdering his brother with an ax—but the man claimed a kid tricked him. The kid he was referring to was a young goat that stubbornly wouldn't leave his farm. According to a September 17, 2006, Associated Press article, the man claimed that he became angry after the animal got his goat and he struck it with an ax. It was then that the goat miraculously turned into his dead brother.

G

James Prusci, an auto repairman with Tires Plus in Winona, Minnesota, told authorities that a woman came into his store and claimed that there was a live animal in her trunk. She explained that she planned to butcher and eat the animal but that her car had broken down on her way to St. Paul. When Prusci opened the truck he was not only surprised to see a live goat, the *Winona Daily News* reported, but also to see that the goat was painted purple and gold, the Minnesota Vikings colors, and had the number "4" (Brett Favre's number) shaved into its side. An animal control vehicle and two police cruisers arrived just as the woman was preparing to drive away with her goat of many colors.

According to a June 12, 2003, Reuters article, Eldon, Oklahoma, resident Pearl Lynne Smith allegedly shot her husband to death during an altercation over who was responsible for feeding the couple's goats.

The *San Francisco Chronicle* reported on July 17, 1997, that a grievance had been filed against Mills College, an eight-hundred-student women's institution, by the Teamsters Local 70 in Oakland, California, citing a violation of an agreement. The teamsters claimed the school contracted nonunion workers to clear about forty acres of poison ivy–infested land, and they demanded restitution. The union stipulated that the school be forced to award back pay for the members who lost out on the work or, as an alternative, that the five hundred nonunion workers who cleared the field be forced to join Local 70. The five hundred nonunion individuals in question were unable to answer these charges, as they were goats. Seriously, the five hundred goats that cleared the land were hired from a company called "Goats R Us." I'm still not sure what the union was thinking; I mean, where are the goats going to keep their union card anyway?

"PORTUGUESE SHEPHERD SHORT-CHANGED IN GOATS-FOR-WIFE DEAL"

—AGENCE FRANCE-PRESSE HEADLINE, SEPTEMBER 18, 2004

G

In September 2002, the *Bay Area Reporter* uncovered that Makinka Moye, who was running for city supervisor in San Francisco, had been arrested earlier that year for beating a goat to death and then butchering its carcass in a vacant lot near a city recreation center.

Hey, with so many barbecues that political candidates must attend, they've got to get the meat from somewhere, right?

According to a May 28, 2009, article in the *Brisbane Courier-Mail*, Mitsubishi Motors, as an incentive for people to buy their new Triton compact pickup, which they deemed as "hardy, versatile units," offered New Zealand farmers a bonus with each truck—a "hardy, versatile" goat.

A seventy-six-year-old Baptist minister from Clarksville, Tennessee, was trying to pull his goat back into a fenced-in pen on his property when the billy goat got a little too gruff. Apparently, the stubborn goat fought the slipknot and began bucking wildly while the minister held on. The rope wound itself around the minister's neck and feet, and he was blue by the time his wife found him. According to a March 19, 2008, article in the *Clarksville Leaf Chronicle*, paramedics declared the minister dead on arrival.

goats

An August 4, 2007, Reuters article reported that Nepal Airlines, which was having continuing technical troubles with one of its two Boeing 757s, announced that it had corrected the problem by sacrificing two goats to placate the Hindu sky god Akash Bhairav.

"It's really bad to think they would do that to innocent animals. I mean, if they have a problem with me, come to me. I have all of my vehicles up here and they didn't touch anything," said Evan Bellin, a Clearfield County, Pennsylvania, farmer. Bellin was complaining about finding that three of his goats had been vandalized; someone had spray painted obscenities on them. According to a May 15, 2008, report on Pittsburgh's WPXI-TV, Bellin was more angry over the affront to him and not the fact that the vandalism will cost him hundreds of dollars, as the wool on the defiled cashmere goats will take months to grow out. He planned to keep the goats in his house.

G

goats

Jen Vrana, president and founder of the Liberty Gay Rodeo Association, is determined to prove that gays and lesbians can be just as macho as straights. In the May 2008 contest held in Devon, Pennsylvania, competitors participated in steer riding, calf roping, and, of course, goat dressing. According to Vrana, in goat dressing, contestants compete to "put hot-pink underwear on the hind quarters of an uncooperative goat in the shortest time." Vrana defended the goat dressing contest by saying, "This is an all-American sport, and we are all-American people [which] proves that we are normal."

As reported in a June 18, 2000, Associated Press article, Nexia Biotechnologies, located outside Plattsburgh, New York, successfully bred 150 goats with a gene from a spider to produce "BioSteel." The company has since been researching ways to use the goat milk with recombinant silk proteins to produce an extraordinarily strong and lightweight silk fiber to use in aerospace and medical applications as well as in bulletproof clothing.

god

"**W**hen I read it, I was taken aback," said the lawyer representing the Federal National Mortgage Association. The attorney was talking about a response from two customers refusing to pay their $54,000 mortgage even though they were facing foreclosure. The married couple claimed they didn't have to pay the money and they got that from the highest source possible—God. "It was our desire to be free from this mortgage debt," the couple told a court handling their foreclosure. "Therefore we asked God our Heavenly Father in the name of Jesus Christ. He heard us and he freed us from this mortgage bondage."

I know God had Moses tell the Pharisees, "Let my people go." I don't remember him saying, "Let my people go debt free."

It is illegal in Vermont to
deny the existence of God.
Atheists can be fined up to $200.

"The man shouted 'God will save me, if he exists,' lowered himself by a rope into the enclosure, took his shoes off, and went up to the lions," stated a zoo official in Kiev, Ukraine, about a June 4, 2006, incident. Thinking it was dinner and a show, "A lioness went straight for him," the official continued, "knocked him down, and severed his carotid artery."

We all, at one point or another, have wanted to blame other people for our problems. Well, a Pennsylvania man took that one step further when he filed a lawsuit claiming someone else is responsible for his problems—God. The man claimed that God the Almighty failed to bring him justice in a thirty-year-old legal battle with his former employer. In his claim, he stated "Defendant God is the sovereign ruler of the universe and took no corrective action against extremely serious wrongs, which ruined [my] life."

He probably thought he would hedge his bets by including a few other codicils just in case he was victorious. In addition to accepting that he is responsible for the man's failures in life, God was also required to return the man's youth and bestow upon him the guitar-playing skills equal to that of Eric Clapton, B. B. King, and other guitar greats. And while God was doing that he could also resurrect the man's mother and pet pigeon. For some reason, a judge threw the case out before it even got a hearing. My guess is that the judge realized that God wasn't a resident of Pennsylvania or even a citizen of the United States and therefore couldn't be called into court. Or am I just talking crazy?

G

god

Is there a jail strong enough to hold God? It's not really a theological question—and the answer is "yes." Ubiquitous Perpetuity God, who used to go by the less ostentatious name Enrique Silberg, was arrested for exposing himself at a coffee shop and sentenced to nine months in jail. However, the sentencing judge said that God could be released to a mental health facility if one agreed to admit him. If God were admitted to a psychiatric hospital, it would certainly make the patients with delusions of grandeur feel pretty foolish.

golf

G

Scott Browning of Houston, Texas, was awarded $16,500 in damages in 1996 from the Men's Club in Houston. Browning ruptured his Achilles tendon during a club-sponsored golf tournament when an exotic dancer assigned to be his "designated caddie" and cart driver got so drunk she overturned their cart into a drainage canal.

Charles Wayne Brown of Newton, Iowa, was hit in the right eye by an errant golf ball stroked by car salesman Bill Samuelson in 1982. Brown's eye was permanently damaged, and he sued Samuelson for failing to yell "fore" before he hit the ball. The lawsuit was dismissed in 1984.

G

golf

Charleston, West Virginia, native Diana J. Nagy filed a lawsuit against the makers of a golf cart for contributing to the death of her husband. Mr. Nagy, who had been drinking heavily during a golf tournament at the Berry Hills Country Club, fell out of the cart to his death. Nagy claimed negligence on the part of the cart manufacturer for not having seat belts and doors in their carts. She also named her son in the lawsuit, who was driving the cart at the time.

Tom Stafford of Mission Viejo, California, sliced a ball too hard to the left, causing it to ricochet off a steel pole and crack him in the forehead. He sued the golf course for damages and, in November 1993, won an $8,500 settlement.

gophers

Two janitors working at a Ceres, California, school were hospitalized and sixteen pupils were injured in a failed attempt by the janitors to kill a gopher. After catching the gopher the two janitors decided the best way to kill him would be by pouring a gum- and wax-removing compound on him, which they did. After the ordeal, one of the janitor needed a break and lit a cigarette. Bad move. The gopher exploded, causing injuries to the janitors, the students, and, of course, the gopher.

government

After his defeat in his congressional race, Arkansas secretary of state Bill McCuen challenged the results of the election with a lawsuit. His suit claimed irregularities in the voting process. The twist is, since vote administration in Arkansas is under the control of the secretary of state's office, McCuen was forced to file the lawsuit against himself.

A according to a report from KOMO-TV in Seattle, the Washington Supreme Court ruled that the city had improperly charged water customers for two years in a row for servicing hydrants when the money should have come from general tax funds. The court ordered the city's customers to receive a $45 refund. However, Seattle discovered that they wouldn't be able to cover the cost of the refunds as they didn't have enough money in the general fund to pay for hydrant services. They figured they could cover the costs by charging customers a $59 surcharge. Television reporters uncovered that the primary reason the city didn't have the money was because they spent $4.2 million on attorneys who filed the account-shuffling lawsuit.

G

government

A supervisor at the Montana Department of Public Health and Human Services told the *Billings Gazette* on March 31, 2008, that a number of his employees were complaining because their newly installed computers lacked certain programs that the workers had grown use to: solitaire, hearts, and Minesweeper. There were also complaints because the workers who had older computers were still able to play the games.

> "Now he's liable to get the sympathy vote."
>
> —MORRISTOWN, NEW JERSEY, TOWN COUNCIL CANDIDATE DONALD CRESITELLO IN OCTOBER 1996 ON HIS CLOSE RACE WITH GEORGE BURKE—AFTER BURKE HAD JUST DIED

B irch trees in national forests in Minnesota are being stripped of their bark by lazy campers looking for easy firewood to burn. The U.S. Forest Service was called in and immediately jumped into action. Did they lie in wait and arrest campers stripping the trees? Nope. They sent workers into the woods armed with buckets of whitewash to paint the barkless birches. After the paint was dry a second coat was applied consisting of dark pigments used to imitate bark and—completing the faux fauna—realistic knotholes. Hmmm, knotholes: sounds like a pretty good description of whoever came up with this idea.

"[This is] a place that would be
pretty much like the place that
I would have grown up in, I think,
if I had have grown up here."

—ALAN KEYES, ON THE CHICAGO NEIGHBORHOOD
HE MOVED TO IN ORDER TO QUALIFY AS A CANDIDATE
FOR U.S. SENATE IN ILLINOIS, 2004

G

government

In Chelmsford, Massachusetts, the town council debated in April 2003 whether to open the meeting with the Pledge of Allegiance. The logical problem soon arose that since the council was already in debate they could not technically "open" with the pledge anyway.

> "You bet we might have."
>
> —SENATOR JOHN KERRY (D-MA), WHEN ASKED IF HE WOULD HAVE GONE TO WAR IN IRAQ IF SADDAM HUSSEIN HAD REFUSED TO DISARM, AUGUST 5, 2004

The mayor of North Providence, Rhode Island, Charles A. Lombardi, realized his administration wasn't using a temporary office trailer, so he decided to sell it on eBay. The resulting sale netted the city $1,825 and netted Lombardi a wealth of bad press. You see, the city didn't own the trailer and had been leasing it from a company called William Scottsman for more than five years. The trailer had the company's name and phone number printed in large type on at least two sides and now has demanded the city reimburse them $11,000—the cost of a new trailer. "I'm not embarrassed," insists Mayor Charles A. Lombardi. "We sold something we knew we didn't need."

G

government

G

government

When city officials in Edison, New Jersey, heard that the "Exxxotica Expo" had been booked at the New Jersey Expo Center, they jumped into action to prevent the event from occurring. According to a November 5, 2009, article on the Huffington Post, the township council quickly amended its zoning laws to prohibit "any shows or sale of sexually oriented products in gatherings of 100 or more people at any place located within 1,000 feet of a place of public worship, school, playground, hospital, or any child care center, or an area zoned for residential use." Only one problem: There are no places of public worship, schools, playgrounds, hospitals, or child care centers, or areas zoned for residential use, within 1,000 feet of the Expo Center, so the show went on as scheduled.

"The voters have spoken— the bastards."

—MORRIS UDALL, ACKNOWLEDGING HIS LOSS IN THE 1976 PRESIDENTIAL PRIMARY ELECTION

gps

G

An unidentified American was traveling on a vacation through Schwarzenbach, Germany, and, as he was unfamiliar with the town, relied entirely on his car's navigation system. When the GPS told him to take a right turn he turned right—right through the front doors of a supermarket. The car the Vietnam War veteran from Toledo, Washington, was driving during the October 2003 incident didn't stop until it crashed into a row of shelves.

"DOH! MAN STEALS GPS TRACKING DEVICE"

—REGISTER (UK) HEADLINE, SEPTEMBER 4, 2003

G

While visiting Bedford Hills, New York, a computer technician from Silicon Valley adhered to his car's GPS so trustingly that he wound up on the tracks of the Metro-North train. Unfortunately, the man's car stalled on the tracks, but he was able to bail out of the car shortly before a train obliterated it.

According to a June 16, 2010, article in the *San Diego Union-Tribune*, a California state law requires that if a sex offender's GPS tagging device indicates that he's in a prohibited area he will face immediate arrest. However the simple law isn't so simple to implement because, as the newspaper investigation reported, the state has fallen roughly 31,000 responses behind.

Jeffrey S. Barber explained to police officers in the town of Tonawanda, New York, that he was simply following the directions from his GPS and wound up in the Niagara River. Apparently Barber's GPS told him to take a right to get to the highway but instead of going on the on-ramp he turned onto an access road, which led to a boat dock, and he didn't stop until he splashed into the river. His explanation was plausible but what police couldn't understand was why the man was walking around in a soggy cow suit. Divers found the car at the bottom of the river along with the head of his cow suit. They also uncovered some possible reasons for Barber's accident: four whiskey bottles and three beer bottles. According to an October 27, 2009, article in the *Lockport Union-Sun & Journal*, Barber was booked for drunken driving after registering a .20 blood alcohol level.

G

gps

headlines

"AND YOU THOUGHT THE NUMBER 666 WAS BAD NEWS"

—San Francisco Chronicle, February 23, 2007

"SHOOTING REPORTED AT FIRING RANGE"

—State newspaper of Columbia, South Carolina, August 4, 2006

"PETS: TO COOK, OR NOT"

—Birmingham News, June 8, 2007

"POLICE SAY MAN SANG, WIELDED HATCHET DURING ROBBERY ATTEMPT"

—Hagerstown (MD) Herald-Mail, January 4, 2005

"GRISLY MEXICO FACTORY BREEDS MAN-EATING FLIES"

—Reuters, February 21, 2003

"BLOOD SPRAYS OUT OF SEWER, ON CITY WORKER"

—WCCO.com (Minneapolis, Minnesota),
March 30, 2007

"INDIAN LAWYERS TIE MAN TO TREE, BEAT HIM"

—Reuters, May 31, 2007

"WOMAN GETS PROBATION FOR CHASING KIDS WITH DILDO"

—Pottstown (PA) Mercury, October 20, 2003

"PRINCIPAL ADMITS THROWING EXCREMENT"

—Toronto Star, April 2, 2007

"COPS: MAN PUT DOG FECES IN ENVELOPE WITH PARKING TICKET"

—USA Today, May 8, 2007

"PALM BEACH COUNTY MAN ARRESTED FOR MAKING FALSE TEETH WITHOUT A LICENSE"

—South Florida Sun-Sentinel, April 24, 2007

iguanas

Two Florida police officers decided to follow the operator of a car because he was driving like he was a little green. They tailed the car for nearly two miles before pulling it over and discovering the driver *was* green—he was an iguana. When the officers approached the car they noticed a three-and-a-half-foot iguana at the wheel and an intoxicated John Ruppell slouched down in the driver's seat. The iguana didn't have car insurance but was friends with the gecko from the Geico commercials.

incredible

Twenty-four-year-old Jessica Bruinsma, visiting from Colorado Springs, Colorado, was hiking in the Bavarian Alps, in Germany near the Austrian border, when she fell during a solo hike. Bruinsma suffered several broken ribs and injured her leg and was unable to climb back to the trail or signal for help. Three days later, she noticed a nearby cable used to haul equipment suddenly started moving. She quickly decided to make the "breast" of the situation. She tied her bra to the supply line and watched as it slowly was reeled out of sight. When the bra arrived at a logging camp below, a logger realized it didn't belong to any tufted titmouse and remembered hearing about a lost hiker. A helicopter followed the line and found Bruinsma bruised, battered, broken, and unsupported. "It certainly beats sending up a flare," said a mountain rescue spokesman, according to a June 23, 2008, report in the *Rocky Mountain News*.

Security officers at the River Park Square mall in Spokane, Washington, noticed that the door of a family restroom on the third floor had been locked for more than an hour. Finally they were able to get the occupant to open the door, and when he did they noticed a color copier sitting on the floor and sheets of uncut $10 bills in the trash. According to a June 6, 2008, article in the *Spokane Spokesman-Review*, Calvin Robinson, a nineteen-year-old homeless man, admitted that he had purchased the copier for $100 in the hopes of producing $90 in counterfeit $10 bills to buy some marijuana. "I don't believe he's going to be recruited by NASA," said Spokane County Sheriff's Office sergeant Dave Reagan.

In May 1995, Kevin Weber, then thirty-five, a parolee with two prior convictions for burglary, broke into a closed restaurant in Santa Ana, California, through a vent in the roof. Once inside, he stuffed his pockets with merchandise, returned to the roof, and was promptly arrested. Orange County Superior Court judge Jean Rheinheimer said in October 1995 that California's "three strikes" law left her no choice but to impose a life sentence, with a minimum of twenty-six years to be served.

But Orange County deputy public defender Deborah Barnum disagreed. Barnum claimed Weber's offense should have been considered a misdemeanor. "She could have given him one year. . . . Neither his record nor the crime warrant the life, minimum twenty-six-year sentence." What did Weber do? He stole four cookies from the restaurant. "That's six and a half years per cookie," said Barnum. Murderers get out on early parole and cookie thieves get a life sentence—that's why it's called just "desserts."

incredible

An English woodcutter from Nayland, Suffolk, split a log and was amazed to discover more than just rings—he also found hands. Fred Crisell discovered a Seiko watch that apparently the cedar tree had grown around over several years.

"It was the most incredible thing I have ever seen in my life. I just could not believe my eyes when I saw where it had been. It is anyone's guess how the watch got into the tree, but it must have been in there several years for the wood to surround it. Unfortunately, the watch does not work but if you shake it you can hear a sort of ticking noise." The watch stopped at 5:26 on a Sunday, the twenty-ninth day of the month (but no one is sure of the year). According to the May 17, 2001, article in the *Daily Mail*, a spokesman for Seiko UK said that serial numbers on the back of the watch showed that it was made in 1987.

A knife-wielding robber of a New York deli was about to make his getaway with a bottle of beer when Rosa Dela Cruz, a worker at the restaurant, demanded he give her the knife. "I got angry. I said 'What are you doing with that knife?'" said Dela Cruz. "Give me that knife! Give me that knife!'" The robber agreed to her demands and threw the knife at her. Amazingly, Dela Cruz somehow managed to grab the knife by the handle, stopping it just inches from her face. The forty-two-year-old Dela Cruz then ordered the stunned robber out of her deli before calling police. The assailant was arrested outside the store and charged with robbery.

"We think she's a ninja," said Detective Lieutenant Tom Fitzpatrick. "She was very calm and cool when we spoke to her. It's incredible she wasn't hurt."

incredible

Jerome Bartens from Haverfordwest, Pembrokeshire, in Wales, was diagnosed deaf in his right ear when he was two years old and struggled in school afterward. But according to a January 28, 2008, article in the *Daily Mail*, while Bartens, then eleven years old, was playing pool with his friends in a church hall, he suddenly felt a pop in his right ear. When he looked down he was amazed to find the tip of a cotton swab that had obviously been lodged in his ear for nearly ten years. "It was just incredible—his hearing returned to normal in an instant. He was cured as suddenly as he became deaf. I had always suspected Jerome had stuck something in his ear when he was little and that was causing the problem. But the doctors and hearing specialists said it was wax and he would probably grow out of it," said Jerome's father, Carsten Bartens. "I am amazed they didn't spot something as obvious as a cotton wool bud."

insurance

In 1992, Gary P. Miller was arrested on insurance-fraud charges in Los Angeles. In April 1994, Miller sued Equitable Life Assurance Society, claiming that since the time of his arrest he had suffered an allergic reaction to courthouses and, as a result, had been unable to continue work at his profession—as a lawyer. Miller stated that exposure to courtrooms, and other aspects of the criminal-justice system, caused him stress, mood swings, and physical sickness. Equitable Life Assurance Society paid him $85,000 as a disability payment. Wait a minute; I thought it was called the criminal *justice* system?

Fletcher Bell, former insurance commissioner of Kansas, hurt himself trying to lift his briefcase from his car trunk. Even though he missed no work or even a golf game on account of the injury, he was awarded $95,000 because of the work-related injury.

insurance

Before insurance companies release a dime for any accident, they check the motorist's statements given at the time the accident occurred. Understandably, motorists are sometimes confused following an accident, and meaning to say something isn't always saying what you mean . . . if you know what I mean. Here are actual explanations from insurance company forms, first published in the *Toronto Sun* on July 26, 1977.

"I thought my window was down but found it up when I put my head through it."

"The guy was all over the road. I had to swerve a number of times before I hit him."

"I had been driving my car for forty years when I fell asleep at the wheel and had an accident."

"To avoid hitting the bumper of the car in front, I struck the pedestrian."

"I told the police that I was not injured, but on removing my hat, I found that I had a skull fracture."

"The pedestrian had no idea what direction to go, so I ran over him."

- - - - - - - - - - - - - - - - - - - -

insurance

"I saw the slow-moving, sad-faced old gentleman as he bounced off my car."

- - - - - - - - - - - - - - - - - - - -

"I was thrown from my car as I left the road. I was later found in a ditch by some stray cows."

- - - - - - - - - - - - - - - - - - - -

"I was unable to stop in time and my car crashed into the other vehicle. The driver and passengers then left immediately for a vacation with injuries."

- - - - - - - - - - - - - - - - - - - -

irony

Police in Denton, Texas, were on the lookout for a man who visited a local tattoo parlor and had a design inked onto his arm. When the job was finished, the man attempted to pay the $200 fee with his credit card, the card was declined, and the man bolted out of the establishment. Police were looking for a man with a newly inked tattoo of praying hands with the motto "Only God Can Judge Me."

Convicted murderer Michael Anderson Godwin was originally sentenced to die in the electric chair but, after years of appeals, got his sentence reduced to life in prison. In 1983, while sitting in his cell at the Central Correctional Institution in Columbia, South Carolina, Godwin attempted to fix a pair of earphones connected to his television set. While sitting on the steel toilet in his cell, Godwin stripped the earphone wire with his teeth and electrocuted himself.

irony

"CANDLES RECALLED BECAUSE OF FLAME RISK"

—ASSOCIATED PRESS HEADLINE, MARCH 28, 2005

A thirty-four-year-old man survived a single-car rollover accident in Nelson, California, according to a May 25, 2009, article in the *Sacramento Bee*. He was able to free himself from the wreck and walked away unharmed. But minutes later, as he was crossing a set of railroad tracks, he was struck and killed by an Amtrak train.

A man referred to by a spokesman for the Vienna, Austria, police as "very religious," had been trapped in an elevator "and had prayed for release." Forty-five-year-old Gunther Link, according to police spokesman Roman Hahslinger, "was pulled out of the elevator and he went straight to the church to thank God." Link was found the next day by parishioners attending mass at the Weinhaus Church, where he had apparently embraced a pillar holding an 860-pound stone altar, which fell on him, killing him instantly.

"CREMATORY CONSUMED BY FIRE"

—CHATTANOOGA TIMES FREE PRESS HEADLINE, MAY 5, 2007

A man in Eureka, California, was caught on surveillance cameras stealing coins from a soda vending machine. Apparently thirsty after stealing all the cold, hard cash, the man put some of the change back into the machine to get a drink. The soda machine malfunctioned and didn't dispense his soda. Outraged at the machine and how it had "eaten his money," the thief, still on tape, mind you, wrote a note on the machine with his name and phone number and the amount of money the machine owed him. I wonder if during his arraignment he paid his bond entirely in quarters.

irony

A thena Sidlar, a trainee at the Allentown, Pennsylvania, State Hospital, was caught helping a mental patient swallow metal objects. According to an August 28, 2009, article in the *Allentown Morning Call*, it was soon uncovered that Sidlar herself has a history of compulsive metal swallowing.

J justice

Oklahoma rapist Darron Bennalford Anderson received a 2,200-year sentence in a Tulsa court in 1994, but was awarded a new trial. Things didn't work out as Anderson had hoped, however, and during his 1996 trial he was resentenced and an additional ninety centuries was tagged on to his sentence (making his term a total of 11,200 years: 4,000 for rape, 4,000 for sodomy, 1,700 years for kidnapping, 1,000 years for burglary and robbery, and 500 years for grand larceny). According to a July 24, 1997, article in the *Dallas Morning News*, Anderson got great news that year after the state Court of Criminal Appeals dismissed the grand larceny charge, as double jeopardy on the robbery conviction, knocking 500 years off his sentence and speeding Anderson's release date to AD 12744.

In 1984, a Texas District Court judge sentenced a thirty-one-year-old Houston man to thirty-five years in prison—for stealing a twelve-ounce, two-dollar can of Spam.

Gilbert Franklin Rhodes, convicted of first-degree murder, was sentenced to serve the rest of his natural life in New Mexico's Department of Corrections—followed by two years parole.

Joseph Shepard, Sr., stayed in a St. Louis–area lockup for more than two years, confident that his lawyer, Michael Kelly, was working hard to get him released on bond after his arrest on drug charges. According to a September 2, 2008, article in the *St. Louis Post-Dispatch*, Shepard's lawyer hadn't done anything in the two years. Shepard seemed naively excited when a reporter looked into his case and petitioned for his release. After the reporter told Shepard he would soon be released, Shepard replied, "If I just sit here long enough, something's going to happen." Three days later, federal judge Carol Jackson released Shepard and chastised Kelly.

J

The highest bail ever set was on Jeffrey Marsh, Juan Mercado, Yolanda Kravitz, and Alvin Kravitz, who were accused of armed robbery. On October 16, 1989, the presiding judge, David L. Tobin, and the four defense attorneys at the Dade County Courthouse in Miami, Florida, set their bail at $100 billion.

In 2003, Michael Peterson was convicted of murdering his wife with a fireplace poker and sentenced to life in prison after a fourteen-week trial in Durham, North Carolina. But Peterson's former neighbor, Larry Pollard, is convinced that the jury was wrong. He believes Mrs. Peterson was killed by an evil owl. According to an August 21, 2008, article in the *Raleigh News & Observer*, Pollard has supplied volumes of information about owls to support his theory but admitted that investigators have found no feathers at the scene of the crime. The State Bureau of Investigation eventually disclosed that they discovered one "microscopic feather" on a clump of hair found in Mrs. Peterson's hand. "[T]he feather has been found," exclaimed Pollard. Investigators hypothesize that the feather, however, is simply an insignificant particle of household down.

A ccording to a July 12, 2008, article in the
Moncton Times & Transcript, an unnamed guest
at the Delta Beausejour hotel in Moncton, New
Brunswick, had continuously postponed a court
date. He decided he would be a no-show again
and asked the concierge to inform the judge of
his absence. When the concierge returned, he
told the guest that the judge wished to inform
his "client" that he had been found guilty on all
counts.

In May 1995, Leon Taylor,
convicted of murdering
a man during a 1994
robbery in Kansas City,
Missouri, was sentenced to
death, plus life in prison,
with an additional 315 years
tacked on.

K | kilts

The New Hampshire House of Representatives debated a controversial bill to make it illegal to discriminate against transgender people (who identify with the sex other than their own). When the votes were tallied on April 8, 2009, the legislation passed by one vote. Interestingly, April 8 was also the state's celebration of Tartan Day, so lawmakers of Scottish ancestry wore kilts to work. Therefore, according to an April 9, 2009, article in the *Concord Monitor*, some opponents of giving greater protection to men who choose to wear skirts instead of pants were wearing skirts that day themselves.

The traditional Scottish garment, the kilt, isn't as traditional as one might think. It was actually invented around 1727 by Thomas Rawlinson, an Englishman. Rawlinson owned an ironworks and thought that the real traditional Highland Scots outfit, a plaid knee-length garment belted at the waist, interfered with efficiency. The garment was cumbersome and looked like a blanket draped around men's bodies—in fact, the Gaelic word "plaid" means "blanket." Rawlinson encouraged his workers to wear his new design by wearing it himself, and soon the fad caught on. Things went so well, in fact, that Parliament banned the kilt in 1745 as a threat to the British way of life. After that, every Scot had to have one in their wardrobe.

ladders

CSX railroad police watched as a thirty-year-old Nashville, Tennessee, man placed a twenty-foot ladder across two different train tracks and waited for a train to come along. The police removed the ladder before a calamity could happen and promptly arrested the man. When asked why he had put the ladder on the tracks in the first place, the man explained that he had stolen the ladder and found it too cumbersome—so he put it on the tracks in hopes a train would come by and make two ten-foot ladders out of it. He was sentenced to six months in jail (or one-half of a one-year sentence).

On March 1, 1992, Los Angeles County police were summoned by a 911 emergency call to Ricks Liquor store on a complaint about a break-in. Police arrived to find twenty-three-year-old Robert W. Laughton alone in the locked store. "When they got there, they could see him sitting on the floor by the front counter, smoking a cigarette and drinking a beer," said Sergeant John O'Neal. Police quickly surmised that Laughton had cut a hole in the ceiling and entered the building through the air ducts.

"After a few minutes, he realizes he can't get back out. So what do you think he does? He calls 911," Los Angeles police sergeant Roger Ferguson said. "[Police officers] yelled to him, and he said he got in through the roof," said Ferguson. "They asked him why he didn't get a ladder from the storeroom. And then he was like 'Oh, yeah. A ladder.'" Knowing this guy's luck he would probably be one rung short anyway.

L

ladders

Apparently Texas farmers about seventy-five miles from the Mexican border near Falfurrias were on their last rung when it came to illegal immigrants making holes in their fences. They decided to install ladders to help the illegals gain entry to the United States. The farmers resorted to this not so much to help the aliens but to keep them from cutting holes in their fences and letting their cattle out. Unfortunately, according to a June 17, 2006, Associated Press article, the ladders were not being used because the border crossers believed them to be some sort of trap.

According to an April 5, 2009, article in the *Daily Mail*, new regulations from the Bedfordshire and Luton Fire and Rescue Service require the use of long poles to test hard-to-reach fire alarms because allowing firefighters to use stepladders might lead to injuries.

A n oversized flag of St. George will no longer fly outside Bourne Town Hall on St. George's Day because of a decision by the South Kesteven District Council in the United Kingdom. According to a May 21, 2009, article in the *Evening Telegraph*, the council is fearful about the "risk" involved in continuing to hoist the flag over a spiked gate using an eight-foot ladder.

L

ladders

Seventy-three-year-old Anthony Gower-Smith sued the Hampshire County Council after he fell off a six-foot stepladder at a primary school near Romsey, Hampshire, where he worked as a janitor. Gower-Smith admitted in court that over the previous thirty years he had frequently used similar ladders without accident and even ticked a box acknowledging he had received "ladder training." He countered by saying, "When you are given something to sign by your superior you just sign it."

On June 17, 2008, the *Sun* reported that, although Gower-Smith told police at the accident site that he had been standing on the top of the ladder and that the accident was his fault, he later claimed, "I don't remember what I said. I was dazed." The court determined that that was a good enough reason to judge him only 25 percent at fault. Since he was claiming up to £50,000, he could receive up to £37,500 in damages.

laughter

L

D amnoen Saen-um, an ice-cream truck driver in the Phrae Province in Thailand, 305 miles north of Bangkok, died while laughing in his sleep. Saen-um's wife claimed her husband laughed for about two minutes, during which time she tried unsuccessfully to wake him, the *Nation* reported on August 20, 2003. "I have never seen a case like this," said Dr. Somchai Chakrabhand, deputy director-general of the Thailand Mental Health Department. "But it is possible that a person could have heart seizure while laughing or crying too hard in their sleep," he said.

A technical support assistant overheard a coworker speaking with a client on the phone. It was apparent that the man on the other end of the phone was having a problem getting his network card working. After several minutes of questions the coworker put the phone on hold and started laughing hysterically. He turned to the tech support assistant and said, "I don't believe it. This guy's complaining that his network card isn't working. The idiot said the card was too long for his expansion slot—so he sawed off the end!"

On March 24, 1975, fifty-year-old bricklayer Alex Mitchell, from King's Lynn, Norfolk, in England, died laughing while watching the "Kung Fu Kapers" episode from the British comedy television series *The Goodies*. After twenty-five minutes of continuously laughing at a kilt-clad Scotsman battling a vicious black pudding with his bagpipes, Mitchell gave one last "tremendous belly laugh, slumped on the settee, and died," said his widow. Mrs. Mitchell, it was reported, later sent a fan letter to *The Goodies* thanking them for making Mitchell's final moments of life so pleasant.

Chrysippus of Soli was a Greek Stoic philosopher (Stoicism is a philosophy that believes that destructive emotions are the result of errors in judgment) who died laughing during the 143rd Olympiad (208–204 BC) at the age of seventy-three. An accounting of his death was given by Diogenes Laërtius, who claimed that Chrysippus was watching a donkey eat some figs and yelled out, "Now give the donkey a drink of pure wine to wash down the figs," whereupon he died in a fit of laughter. Chrysippus was succeeded as head of the Stoic school by his pupil Zeno of Tarsus.

L

laughter

L the law

In Alaska it is against the law to "disturb a grizzly bear in order to take its picture."

"Speed upon country roads will be limited to ten miles an hour unless the motorist sees a bailiff who does not appear to have had a drink in thirty days, then the driver will be permitted to make what he can."

—EL DORADO COUNTY, CALIFORNIA, LAW

Mississippi common law states that "every citizen has the right to shoot to kill if necessary when escorting a woman home from a quilting party and another man interferes and threatens to shoot him."

The law in Logan County, Colorado, forbids a man to kiss a woman "while she is asleep, without first waking her."

the law

The law in Groton, Connecticut, states that "any utterances from a man in a bow tie are not to be credited."

"No male person shall make remarks to or concerning, or cough or whistle at, or do anything to attract the attention of any woman upon traveling along any of the sidewalks."

—ABILENE, TEXAS, LAW

"Bathing in the state of nudity in the water within the corporate limits of this Village" states a Spring Valley, New York, law, is forbidden between the hours of 5 a.m. and 8:30 p.m.

L

the law

There is an unusual law in Buckfield, Maine, regarding when you should and should not pay a taxicab driver. The ordinance decrees that no taxi driver "will be allowed" to ask for, or charge, a fare to any passenger who gives him "sexual favors" in exchange for a lift home. The law goes on to specify that the person who grants the sexual favor must be leaving an "establishment which serves alcoholic beverages," or any "place of business" which sells liquor. Even then the cab driver will probably still expect a tip.

"No maternity hospital shall receive an infant without its mother, except in cases of emergency."

—Colorado state statute

"Shoes are required to eat in any restaurant or other place serving food to the public."

—Strangely phrased law from Redding, California

"Any services performed by a jackass must be recorded."

—Law in Baltimore, Maryland

"A one-armed piano player may be seen, but not if admission is charged to view his performance."

—Iowa law

the law

According to Oklahoma common law: "Insanity is not evidenced when a widow, anxious to marry, shows her love letters from one suitor to another, and boasts constantly about her conquests, both real and those imagined."

It is against the law in Connecticut to sell pickles that, when dropped one foot from the ground, break or become soft. "They should remain whole and even bounce."

lawsuits

A street artist who worked in the West End of Dallas, Texas, peddled a pretty exclusive style of art—or so he thought. Krandel Lee Newton's specialty was drawing people's buttocks. He was the bottom line in butt sketching and even trademarked his business name, "Butt Sketch." But in 1992, another street artist, Mark Burton, rear-ended Newton's line of artistic expression and also began drawing pictures of people's bottoms. Burton gave his business the name "Fanny Sketch."

Newton wasn't going to turn the other cheek on this intrusion into his livelihood; he filed a federal lawsuit accusing Burton of threatening his business. Burton soon realized he would get his butt kicked in court and decided to settle with Newton. Burton promised to stop using the name "Fanny Sketch" and to discontinue doing posterior portraits that might cause people to confuse his work with Mr. Newton's. I'm sure if Newton had taken Burton to trial, a good prosecutor would have found a crack in the case.

L

lawsuits

In the mid-'80s, bank president Michael Brennan of St. Paul, Minnesota, needed to relieve himself and stepped into the executive washroom of his own bank. Michael sat on the toilet seat and completed his business. When he flushed the toilet, however, he nearly hit the roof. A geyser with "two hundred to three hundred gallons" of raw sewage "came blasting up out of the toilet with such force it stood him right up," according to Brennan's attorney. Without notifying the bank, a construction company had shut off a nearby sewer line, causing pressure to build up in the pipes. Brennan sued both the city and the construction company for $50,000, citing the "humiliation and embarrassment" he suffered when his accident became public. The jury was sympathetic to Brennan's plight but told him he was crap out of luck on any settlement. The construction company did, however, offer to buy Brennan a new suit.

Jeffrey Fennell was intoxicated when he decided to grab his assault rifle and start shooting up his house in Ventura, California. Police quickly arrived on the scene, and when Fennell saw them he began shooting at them, too. The ensuing four-hour shoot-out finally ended when a SWAT officer shot Fennell in the shoulder. No one else was wounded in the melee, and Fennell was arrested and taken into custody. His wife, Julie Greenleaf, filed claims with the city demanding nearly $700,000, which included $759 for bullet holes in her house (caused when officers returned fire), $32,000 for her husband's medical bills, and $650,000 for future medical expenses and loss of earnings. After police called the claims "ludicrous" and refused to pay, Greenleaf reduced the claim to $250.

L

ontrose, Iowa, native Betty Boulton filed a thirty-dollar lawsuit in the late 1980s against her neighbor, E. M. Chadwick. In her complaint, Boulton claimed Chadwick's beagle, Murphy, tore a hole in her screen door and impregnated her little Scottish terrier. Boulton sought damages for the cost of an abortion. "She [Boulton] came up here asking me to pay for an abortion," said Chadwick about the complaint. "I told her I didn't think Murphy was the father. If he is the father, I think we should have some say on whether she should have had an abortion without consulting Murphy or myself. I'm opposed to abortion."

eigh Ann Fisher, a high school student in Vilonia, Arkansas, along with her parents, filed a $4.2 million lawsuit in August 1992 against Leigh Ann's school. The lawsuit claimed "emotional distress" after Leigh Ann was replaced as captain of her cheerleading squad. "Sis, boom, bah!" said the judge—the case was dropped. Rah, rah, rah!

University of Idaho freshman Jason Wilkins
thought it would be funny to moon his
friends from a third-story dormitory window.
The eighteen-year-old climbed on top of a three-
foot-high radiator, dropped his pants, and pressed
his butt against the window—which promptly
shattered. Wilkins suffered four fractured
vertebrae, abrasions to his hands, and "deeply
bruised buttocks" from the fall out the window.
After he picked himself up off the concrete, the
embarrassed Wilkins said, "This is just a freak
accident." But six months after the accident,
Wilkins had a change of heart. He and his
parents sued school officials, claiming they were
negligent for failing to warn dorm residents of
"the danger associated with upper-story windows."
They asked for $940,000 in damages—that's
$470,000 per cheek, in case you were wondering.
The claim was denied. "We've got a kid that's
presumably of average intelligence with his bare
bottom against a window, leaning back," said Al
Campbell, claims manager for the state's Bureau
of Risk Management. "That doesn't seem very
bright to me."

L

lawsuits

The Wawa food store chain, which controls five hundred outlets in five states, demanded that the lone Haha market in eastern Pennsylvania change its name. In their lawsuit filed in late 1996, Wawa claimed that Haha is too similar in sound and could confuse people into believing that Haha is affiliated with Wawa. Haha owners Tamilee and George Haaf, Jr., claimed they have a right to use the name since it is simply an abbreviation of their last name. They originally considered "Haaf and Haaf" as the name of their market but settled on Haha instead. Wawa claimed that Haha's defense is poo-poo.

lawyers

Mark Kirby, a bankruptcy lawyer from Raleigh, North Carolina, was indicted on federal fraud charges in December 1993. In 1990 and 1991, while Kirby was working for the Brown, Kirby, and Bunch law firm, he billed clients an average of 1,200 hours a month. Why would anyone prosecute such a hardworking attorney? Because a thirty-one-day month only has 744 hours. I've heard of working overtime—but this is outrageous.

The Virginia legislature passed a law in 1658 outlawing lawyers. In case you're wondering, it's no longer on the books.

L

lawyers

In August 1992, attorney Ben Echeverria of Escondido, California, filed a $2 million lawsuit against Texaco, Inc., and a local Escondido gas station manager for discrimination. Echeverria claimed the practice of having gas station attendants pump gas at self-service pumps for female customers was discriminatory against men, who had to pump their own gas. The suit was settled out of court with the gas station agreeing to stop its chivalrous activities, forcing women to pump their own gas themselves.

Richard Jacobs of St. Louis, Missouri, argued that the reason the jury found him guilty of stealing court documents was they had been prejudiced against him. Jacobs claimed he was demonized because the judge allowed the jury to learn his occupation: Jacobs is a lawyer.

A ttorney Jay Rothman filed a lawsuit against a flower shop in the Tarzana neighborhood in Los Angeles in November 1992 for malicious negligence. Rothman had purchased a bouquet of flowers for his wife, who had just given birth to their daughter, and composed a love note to accompany the arrangement. The flower shop lost the note. Rothman refused to settle out of court, claiming the words he had written were unique and that "I'm a hard-nosed, aggressive plaintiff's attorney. [Composing the note was] one of the only times in my life that I was really inspired."

Lawyer James Benfer hurt his back while lifting and inspecting the underside of his leather office chair. He sued for workers' compensation and was awarded $107,913.75.

L

In December 1993, Dennis Scheib, an attorney practicing in Atlanta, Georgia, briefly stopped by the prosecutor's office in the downtown courthouse while en route to meet his newest client. As he was leaving the office, Scheib noticed two police officers in hot pursuit of a man running down the hall. The officers yelled out that the man had escaped them, and they ordered him to stop. Scheib dropped his briefcase and ran with the two officers to help recapture the man. As the police officers slapped the handcuffs on the escapee, Scheib discovered the man was the client he had been assigned to represent in court.

Houston attorney George Fleming, on behalf of dozens of people, sued the manufacturers of defective plastic pipe. The settlement gave the lawyer a fee of nearly $109 million while the customers, who were inconvenienced by the faulty products, received replacement plumbing valued at $1,200. District Judge Russell Lloyd considered Fleming's original fee as "almost scandalous" and reduced it to a mere $43.5 million.

legal

L

An assistant professor of art history at Northwestern University in Evanston, Illinois, collected $33,000 in Social Security checks for his mother before finally notifying the government that his mother had died. He had allowed the checks to be electronically deposited into the joint account he shared with his mother for five years without telling anyone of her passing. The professor's lawyer described his client's actions as "extreme procrastination behavior" brought on by depression following the death of his mother. I'll bet the professor has at least 33,000 reasons for not reporting his mother's death to Social Security officials.

The New York Appellate Division of the Supreme Court unanimously revoked a lower court's award of $15 million to a Richmond Hill High School student who is paralyzed from the waist down. The New York City schoolboy was horsing around before volleyball practice and, when the coach left the auditorium, leaped over the volleyball net and landed on his head, breaking his neck. The student explained why he thought he was entitled to the enormous settlement by saying, "I accept part of the blame, but what about the responsibility of the teacher and the school?"

"When he's sober, he's very much against drinking and driving."

—ATTORNEY FOR THE FOUNDER OF STUDENTS AGAINST DRINKING AND DRIVING AT CALGARY UNIVERSITY, IN RESPONSE TO HIS CLIENT'S SECOND DRUNKEN DRIVING OFFENSE

As reported in the "Police Beat" column of the *Arizona Daily Wildcat*, the University of Arizona student newspaper, a nineteen-year-old student filed a charge against a fellow student accusing him of stealing his fake Arizona driver's license. The complainant confessed that he had loaned the man the card, but after it was confiscated at a local club, the borrower refused to reimburse the complainant the forty dollars he had paid for it. Remember kids, "ID" are the first two letters in the word "idiot"!

Judge Philip Mangones in Keene, New Hampshire, declared unconstitutional a dormitory search of two Keene State College students. The students agreed to allow authorities to search their room and when more than six ounces of marijuana was found, the two students were arrested. The judge ruled in favor of the boys, stating that they were too stoned to know what they were doing when they consented to the search. Sounds like what happens when smoke gets in your eyes.

> "Had I not been born with breasts,
> I would not have been prosecuted.
> It's not for attention. It's for civil rights."
>
> —A TEXAS WOMAN WHO WAS CONVICTED OF
> DISORDERLY CONDUCT AFTER SHE BARED HER BREASTS
> AT SYLVAN BEACH IN LA PORTE

mail M

We've all heard the expression "The check's in the mail." But for 2,600 state employees whose weekly paychecks got lost in the mail, the joke was on them—they were all postal employees. In Norfolk, Virginia, postal employees awaited their last paycheck of the year, eagerly anticipating getting their checks deposited before the banks closed for the holidays. But (ah, delicious irony) the post office lost their own mail. The checks did arrive—two days late and too late for the employees to get to the bank.

"We're sure that the irony will not be lost on folks," said Bruce Threatte, finance director at the Norfolk post office. Where were the checks for those few extra days? No one seems to know. The frightening thing is, at one time, there were 2,600 disgruntled postal employees in one place.

mail

"Going postal" has become part of our lexicon—meaning, of course, someone who becomes violent on the job (named because of the high number of postal employees who lose it at work). One clerk at Denver's downtown terminal annex was escorted from the building after he "exhibited some bizarre behavior . . . besides wearing a dress." Although the clerk was informed he should go home and stay away from the annex, he returned twice that day wearing not only the dress but also a gorilla mask and something authorities described as a strap-on sexual device. The police were called to the scene where they discovered several guns and two hunting knives in the man's pickup truck. Surprisingly, a psychiatric evaluation was ordered.

mail

Christmas is the busiest time of the year for the post office. People mail millions of boxes, cards, and letters to friends and relatives everywhere in the world. It's a happy time, a joyous time. So it came as some surprise to the good people of Ohio when twelve thousand pieces of mail were stamped with an unusual greeting of holiday cheer. Instead of a brightly stamped "Merry Christmas," the Yuletide mail recipients got a Scroogy "You bitch" stamped on their mail, courtesy of their local post office. It gives the expression "Ho, Ho, Ho" a whole new meaning.

M memos

"**B**ecause of the Veterans Day holiday next Wednesday, this release will be published on Friday, November 13, instead of on Thursday, November 12. It will be issued on Thursday, November 19, its usual publication date, but will be delayed the following week until Friday, November 27, because of the Thanksgiving Day holiday on Thursday, November 26."

—FEDERAL RESERVE MEMO

I n 1991, managers of the cafeteria located in the U.S. Treasury Department building issued a memo stating that of the 2,040 individual pieces of silverware it owned, 1,430 pieces were missing and presumed stolen. Among other agencies, the building houses the Internal Revenue Service. But who's counting?

C ommunications is the most important element of any business—especially in this age of worldwide communication and the information superhighway. This memo from the Office of Management and Budget (OMB) gives us a clear picture of how things are done in Washington.

"An agency subject to the provisions of the Federal Reports Act may enter into an arrangement with an organization not subject to the Act whereby the organization not subject to the Act collects information on behalf of the agency subject to the Act. The reverse also occurs."

Sometimes I think aliens have landed and set up shop in our nation's capital.

M | the military

When it comes to the military, "Just the fax, ma'am," isn't good enough. In 1992, Senator Carl Levin (D-MI) checked into reports that the Air Force was buying 172 custom-made fax machines by Litton Industries. These fax machines were specially designed to survive a nuclear blast. But the real blast was the cost—$73 million. After closer scrutiny, Senator Levin realized that these costs were inaccurate; the Air Force was actually spending more than $94 million—or $547,000 per machine. Magnavox put in a bid to the Air Force for fax machines that met the required specifications and cost only $15,000 per unit. But, unfortunately, the Magnavox model transmitted pages in "newspaper" quality while the half-million-dollar Litton fax machine transmitted in "magazine" quality.

> "Funds obligated for military assistance as of September 3, 1979, may, if deobligated, be reobligated."
>
> —Budget of the United States, fiscal year 1980

Two former employees of the Sioux Manufacturing Corporation revealed in a 2006 whistle-blower lawsuit that between 1994 and 2006 the company had been shorting the quality of the Kevlar in more than two million combat helmets sold to the Pentagon. Sioux didn't contest the charges and in February 2008 agreed to pay $2 million to settle the dispute. According to a February 18, 2008, article in the *Air Force Times*, while the Pentagon was still investigating whether the lighter threading in the Kevlar was endangering U.S. troops, the U.S. Air Force nonetheless contracted with Sioux to produce new Kevlar combat helmets.

In 1989, Congress supplied the Pentagon with $49,000 to discover if members of the armed forces would spend money on military lottery tickets.

N names

Arrested for public urination
in Bowling Green, Ohio:
Mr. Joshua Pees.

—Bowling Green Sentinel-Tribune, September 5, 2001

In February 1995, attorney Charles Peruto, Jr.,
was negotiating a low bail for his client in
a Norristown, Pennsylvania, courtroom. Even
though his client, Howard "Wing Ding" Jones,
was an accused drug dealer, Peruto tried to
convince the judge that his client would not
jump bail. The judge didn't believe Peruto's
argument and raised Jones's bail from $1,000 to
$150,000—at which point Jones fled the courtroom.

Charged with possession of
thirty-three pounds of cocaine
in Roseville, Michigan:
Denise Coke.

—Associated Press, May 5, 2005

Finishing thirty-fifth in the
Club North Shore Half Marathon
near Chicago in April 1993 was
thirty-eight-year-old
Mr. Farm Vehicle.

From a "Legal Notice of a Name Change" in the August 24, 2005, issue of the *Honolulu Advertiser*: "Waiaulia Alohi anail ke alaamek kawaipi olanihenoheno Kam Paghmani" changed his name to, "Waiaulia Alohi anail ke alaamek kawaipi olanihenoheno Kam."

The victim of fatal gunshots
in Buffalo, New York:
Mr. Mister Rogers.

—*BUFFALO NEWS*, OCTOBER 26, 2009

Arrested for robbery in Ottawa, Ontario:
Mr. Emmanuel Innocent.

—*OTTAWA SUN*, NOVEMBER 29, 2001

Police officer **Tracy Sixkiller** arrested **Russell Hogshooter** and **Belinda Chewey** after a police chase in Jay, Oklahoma.

—*Tulsa World*, July 2, 2000

In 1990, the Idaho Court of Appeals turned over a case to the trial court to determine if a man's right to privacy had been violated. An undercover officer assigned to a public restroom (to check on complaints of indecent activities) looked over the top of one of the stalls and discovered a man in the midst of masturbation. When the case went to trial it was indexed under the alleged masturbator's name: *State v. Dale D. Limberhand.*

The name of a ninety-year-old man arrested on July 18, 2007, for public indecency: **Leonard Dickman.**

Arrested for exposing himself
in the front window of a
Nashua, New Hampshire, business:
Joseph Dangle.

—*Nashua Telegraph*, December 15, 2000

G athering evidence for a possible charge of
pornography, a Sullivan County, Tennessee,
detective rented four X-rated videos from a local
video store. The two owners of the store were
eventually acquitted and all charges were dropped.
The owners were in no mood to "be kind and
rewind," so they decided to sue the county.
They charged that the detective had returned the
four porno tapes late and they sought a $3,000
settlement. The court ruled in their favor but
awarded only $64 to the store's owners—whose
names were Nancy and Charles Bible.

T he defense attorney for Tyrone Jerrols of
Houston, Texas, who was facing charges
of murder, filed a motion to prevent the use of
Jerrol's nickname, "Hitman," claiming it would
prejudice the jury.

Suing the Oklahoma University law
school for unlawful expulsion:
Mr. Perry Mason.

—*Norman Transcript*, January 11, 2001

Pleaded guilty to bank fraud in
Pine Ridge Oglala Sioux reservation
in South Dakota: **Manuel Fool Head**
and his wife, **Sandra Fool Head.**

—*Sioux Falls Argus Leader*, July 12, 2001

Booked for aggravated assault and
burglary in Salt Lake City, Utah:
Mr. Joe Snot.

—*CrimeReports.com*, January 1, 2002

Charged with stealing tires in Wilkes-
Barre, Pennsylvania: **Edgar Spencer,**
his son **Edgar Spencer, Jr.,** the older
man's brother **Edgar W. Spencer,** and
his son, **Edgar W. Spencer, Jr.**

—*Wilkes-Barre Times Leader*, May 8, 2002

new zealand

People in Tauranga, New Zealand, reported that they saw a semi-naked man speeding down the road with his butt on fire. John Sullivan ended up in court on February 17, 2003, and was sentenced to two hundred hours of community work for driving an unlicensed motorized barstool. Strategically placing a rolled-up newspaper and lighting it caused the flames, Sullivan admitted. He also stated that the motorized barstool can reach speeds of up to 50 mph and on the night in question he had "had a few" at the bar before roaring off into the dark. Sullivan's party trick gives a new dimension to the term "tail pipe."

> "Man Killed in Argument During Scrabble Game"
>
> —NEW ZEALAND HERALD, JULY 15, 2006

N

A female employee and her supervisor went out to a bar in Otautau, New Zealand, to have drinks after work. During the course of the evening the supervisor suddenly dropped to his knees. Was he proposing? Nope, was trying to bite the buttocks of the woman but was unsuccessful because his false teeth fell out before he could get within biting range.

The woman filed a sexual harassment complaint for US$4,175 but was turned down by an employment tribunal. They made their decision based on inconsistencies in the woman's story and the fact that the alleged harassment happened away from the job. We've all had a supervisor that was a pain in the butt, but this guy got carried away.

S ex workers in New Zealand can claim the cost of bubble bath, dairy whip, condoms, lubricants, gels, oils, tissues, lingerie, costumes, and see-through garments against their income tax. It must be great to be a CPA in New Zealand.

nurses

In January 2006 a nurse from Kyoto, Japan, was sentenced to more than three years in prison after she was found guilty of engaging in a bizarre way of relieving work-related stress—tearing off the fingernails and toenails of incapacitated patients.

obsessions

The expression "I can dig it" took on a whole (or hole) new meaning in 2001 when William Lyttle was discovered to have been obsessively digging tunnels underneath his twenty-room house in North London, England. Lyttle had burrowed passed his property line and a cave-in caused a fifteen-foot hole to open up in the street. Five years later, Lyttle, in his midseventies, was temporarily removed from his house when it was found that his mole mania had threatened the integrity of the entire street and, combined with the overwhelming amount of junk he had accumulated, his house was in danger of sinking into the ground.

ordinances

O

An ordinance in Grangeville, Idaho, makes it clear that "no citizen shall allow their turkeys, chickens, cattle, horses, lions, or tigers to be led by chains along a street" in the community.

Morticians in Alabama could lose their licenses if they use "profane, indecent, or obscene language in the presence of a human dead body."

"It is unlawful for any male person within the corporate limits of the City of Ottumwa to wink at any female person with whom he is unacquainted."

—MUNICIPAL CODE OF OTTUMWA, IOWA

"Cab drivers may not knowingly carry a person of questionable or bad character to his or her destination."

—MAGNOLIA, ARKANSAS, ORDINANCE

Sparks, Nevada, ordinance: "A citizen is forbidden to drive a donkey along Main Street in August without a straw hat being worn." But *who* should be wearing the hat?

"Any vehicles meeting at an intersection must stop. Each must wait for the other to pass. Neither can proceed until the other is gone."

—NEW HAMPSHIRE TRAFFIC ORDINANCE

"No person shall halloo, shout, bawl, scream, use profane language, dance, sing, whoop, quarrel, or make any unusual noise or shout in any house in such a manner as to disturb the peace and quiet of the neighborhood."

—JACKSONVILLE, ILLINOIS, ORDINANCE

"Any person who shall wear in a public place any device or thing attached to her head, hair, headgear, or hat, which device or thing is capable of lacerating the flesh of any other person with whom it may come in contact and which is not sufficiently guarded against the possibility of so doing, shall be adjudged a disorderly person."

—SECAUCUS, NEW JERSEY, ORDINANCE

"No person shall disturb the occupant of any house by knocking on the door or ringing the bell. Nor shall a person yell, stomp, pound on, or kick a door to get the attention of the occupant or occupants."

—BRIDGEWATER, NEW JERSEY, ORDINANCE

In Los Angeles, California, it is legal for a man to beat his wife with a strap or leather belt. However, the husband may not strike his wife with a belt wider than two inches unless he has his wife's permission.

O

ordinances

"No young woman shall sit on a man's lap without a cushion or a pillow under her."

—LAWTON, OKLAHOMA, ORDINANCE

"It is prohibited for pedestrians and motorists to display frowns, grimaces, scowls, threatening and glowering looks, gloomy and depressed facial appearances, generally all of which reflect unfavorably upon the city's reputation."

—POCATELLO, IDAHO, ORDINANCE

In New York City, "It is disorderly conduct for one man to greet another man on the street by placing the end of his thumb against the tip of his nose, at the same time extending and wriggling the fingers of his hand."

In Kentucky, "No female shall appear in a bathing suit on any highway within this state unless she be escorted by at least two officers or unless she be armed with a club." However, this Kentucky law goes on to say, "The provisions of this statue shall not apply to females weighing less than 90 pounds nor exceeding 200 pounds nor shall it apply to female horses."

In Pacific Grove, California, according to City Ordinance No. 352, it is a misdemeanor to kill or threaten a butterfly.

An ordinance in Dallas, Texas, forbids "walking about aimlessly, without apparent purpose, lingering, hanging around, lagging behind, idly spending time, delaying, sauntering, and moving slowly about."

"Since the Jasper husband is accountable for his wife's misbehavior, he has the legal right to chastise her with a stick no larger around than his thumb."

—JASPER, ALABAMA, ORDINANCE

A Boston, Massachusetts, ordinance states: "A lodger shall not be lodged for more than seven consecutive nights unless he shall have taken a bath."

outrageous

Fire officials estimated that an unidentified couple in Dartmouth, Massachusetts, had amassed forty-five gallons of gasoline in plastic water jugs in their apartment's utility closet with the intention of using it when the price of gas went up. But the only thing that went up, according to a June 6, 2008, article in the *New Bedford Standard-Times*, was their apartment and seven others that were left uninhabitable. The fire marshal's office determined that the fire was accidental, probably resulting from a spark from the gas water heater.

A grand jury didn't believe the sequence of events that led to the death of a Soldotna, Alaska, man. The accused murderer said he awoke to find his cousin flailing on the floor in mortal agony from a self-inflicted gunshot. And that instead of calling 911 he decided the humane thing to do was to finish him off. He was indicted on charges of first-degree murder.

Larry Nettles, of Charleston, South Carolina, returned from the funeral home clutching a small pink plastic bag he was told contained his deceased father-in-law's personal effects. But it was more personal than Nettles ever thought. Days later, a pungent odor emitted from the closet and the real contents were discovered after the family cat clawed the bag open. "It was him in the bag, not his personal belongings," Nettles said. The funeral home had accidentally given Nettles a medical waste bag used to hold the deceased's heart and other organs that are removed after an autopsy. Nettles contacted the funeral home and was told to simply bury the contents in his backyard. But Nettles, having more guts than most people, threatened a lawsuit if the funeral home didn't give the organs a proper burial.

O

outrageous

O overreacting

Marcus Johnson of Wichita, Kansas, was stopped by an officer and told to lower the volume on his radio. Johnson became so incensed at the demand that he immediately drove to city hall. Not so weird, you say, until you learn he drove up the wheelchair ramp at 45 mph, reported the *Wichita Eagle* on May 21, 2009, smashed through the front door, and drove through the building. He was sentenced to ten years in prison.

Robert Caton and his wife were at a Tesco store in Andover, Hampshire, in England, ordering a new bed. When the salesman quoted them the price he said that the bed did not come with a mattress. According to a May 21, 2009, article in the *Daily Telegraph*, Caton went out to the parking lot, got into his Rolls-Royce, and drove it through the front window of the store.

The *Star Press*, in Muncie, Illinois, reported on June 15, 2009, that Robert Stahl was arrested after getting into an argument with a man in his fifties. He resolved the conflict by reaching into the man's mouth and pulling out his dentures. This was his second conviction in seven months involving the same form of self-defense.

According to a June 28, 2009, article in the *Daily Mail*, retirees who gather weekly to share stories and coffee at the Peterborough public library in the United Kingdom were ordered by the Peterborough City Council to give up their hot drinks for fears that they might accidentally spill one on a child.

The *St. Paul Pioneer Press* reported in their crime column that police were called to the 1300 block of Desoto Street by a forty-three-year-old man who wanted to file a report. According to the July 30, 2009, article, the man wanted to report that he had found a slice of half-eaten pizza near his fence and knew it represented someone's intent to "harass" him.

O
overreacting

Brian Taylor complained to police in Carlisle, Pennsylvania, about a man who had simply flicked a toothpick on the sidewalk. The police cited the fifty-six-year-old toothpick flicker because Taylor explained that the discarded toothpick was deliberately thrown, according to September 22, 2009, article in the *Patriot-News*, in order to "annoy" Taylor.

BBC producers holding a "telephone-book-size" set of safety precautions accosted Sir Robin Knox-Johnston, the first man to single-handedly sail around the globe nonstop, while he was making an adventure documentary. According to an April 18, 2009, *Daily Mail* article, the producers were demanding that the historical adventurer not light a portable stove unless supervised by a "safety adviser."

Gildazio Costa of Framingham, Massachusetts, was arrested and charged with kidnapping and assaulting his girlfriend. According to a February 10, 2009, article in the *Metrowest Daily News*, Costa and his girlfriend had had a five-hour-long argument concerning the operating hours for the local library.

The *Daily Mail* reported on January 24, 2009, that the Happy Egg Company in Lincoln, England, had chosen to alter its carton packaging to include the warning: "Allergy Advice: Contains Egg."

A seventy-two-year-old Levis, Quebec, woman was clearing her walk with a snowblower when some of the snow accidentally landed in her neighbor's yard. According to a December 5, 2007, article in the *Edmonton Sun*, her forty-three-year-old neighbor took it as a personal affront, grabbed his snowblower, and blew some snow back into her yard. The snowblowing blowout lasted about ten minutes and culminated when the neighbor allegedly punched the woman and her husband, who had come out to help. The man was charged with assault.

O

overreacting

Jeremy Bell had just finished putting together a Lego gun from a kit he had received that day. Several of the parts fell off shortly after he put it together, so he stored all the pieces back in their original box and started playing video games with some office mates. Moments later a squad of heavily armed "tactical" police officers burst into his Toronto, Ontario, office and ordered him against the wall. According to a December 4, 2009, article in the *Toronto Sun*, Bell said he wasn't too worried about staring down the barrel of several automatic machine guns. "I'm not trafficking guns or selling drugs or anything like that," Bell said later, "so as soon as I saw that these cops were legit, I was like, all right, this has got to be about this stupid gun." Apparently someone in an apartment complex across the street saw Bell with the gun and alerted the authorities. The man later apologized via Twitter and a note he left on Bell's window: "Sorry, dude, it looked real."

A s reported in an October 5, 2007, article in the *National Post*, the city of Toronto was campaigning with posters and a Web page to urge citizens to vote on a proposition that would set aside a one-cent tax for municipal services. But the Royal Canadian Mint didn't like the city using the likeness of their "registered trademark" (the picture of the penny and the phrase "one cent") and sent the city a bill for about $47,000.

P o Shiu-fong was sentenced to six months in jail in Hong Kong, according to a July 4, 2007, Reuters article, for stabbing her boyfriend in his right eye with a chopstick because she thought he was being unfaithful to her. Shiu-fong admitted at her hearing that, six years earlier, she had blinded her boyfriend in the left eye by poking him with her finger because she believed he was cheating on her.

overreacting

"I don't see why a man can't shoot his own TV if he wants to," said Indianapolis loading-dock worker Bobby Johnson. Johnson was arrested for criminal recklessness after he emptied six bullets into his $900 Zenith television set. The angered Johnson told the *Indianapolis Star* he capped the TV because his forty-one-channel cable TV provider offered him "nothing to watch." And they say Elvis is dead!

pizza | P

According to an April 29, 2008, article in the *Las Cruces (NM) Sun-News*, Adolfo Martinez and Mark Anderson were accused of passing forged checks and indicted for fraud. Their brilliant plan consisted of buying Domino's pizzas with bad checks, then donning Pizza Hut shirts and reselling the pizzas, by the slice, in a local park or in front of stores. They were noticed because even though one of the men was wearing a Pizza Hut shirt they were selling the pizzas out of a Domino's boxes.

In March 1995, Jerry Williams, considered a habitual criminal under California's "three strikes" law, was sentenced to twenty-five years to life. What was the crime that put Williams away for good? He stole a slice of pizza from a group of children on a Redondo Beach pier. Justice is served.

P

pizza

Dispatcher: "911. What is your emergency?"

Male caller: "Yeah, I want to order a pizza."

Dispatcher: "You need to call 411."

When police pulled over William Bethel on April 27, 2006, because his car didn't have an inspection sticker they discovered he was also driving on a suspended license. Police informed Bethel that they were going to impound his car and, during a routine check of the vehicle, they noticed a stretcher, some old clothes, and several pizzas. Bethel told police that he not only used the car to deliver Domino's pizzas but also to transport dead bodies to a local funeral home. According to an article in the *Bucks County Courier Times*, Bethel was not arrested and faces only $400 in fines for driving on a suspended license and not having an inspection certificate. Apparently, using the same vehicle to transport dinner and the dearly departed is not a violation of county ordinances.

In 1999, the General Accounting Office noted that while frozen cheese pizzas were inspected by the Food and Drug Administration, those with meat toppings were inspected by the Department of Agriculture.

The manager of a pizza restaurant in Lakewood, Ohio, was arrested and eventually indicted for stealing $38,000 from the company—not just in dough, mind you, but also in dough. The woman, in an effort to bolster her store's sales figures, fabricated big call-in orders and then took the pizzas home. Not only did her ploy boost sales figures, she also became part of the company's upper crust and had her picture in the company newsletter. She eventually got busted, however, when she asked the pizzeria's owner to help her move to a new house and he discovered more than four hundred rotting, moldy pizzas stacked to the ceiling in a spare room. It's very possible the woman was arrested in thirty minutes or less.

P

pizza

Stephanie Martinez was nervously handing over the money from the Denton Pizza Patron restaurant where she worked to a disguised robber, according to a *Denton Record Chronicle* article from July 15, 2008. Suddenly, a coworker went on the offensive, knocking the robber down and beating him until his sunglasses and wig fell off. Martinez recognized the man at once. "Don't hit him again! That's my dad!" she screamed. Martinez's father, mother, and stepfather were all charged with attempted robbery—but police concluded that Martinez had no knowledge of the robbery and had been kept completely in the dark.

In March 1994, the *Providence Journal-Bulletin* reported that the IRS office in Rhode Island was zeroing in on tax underpayments by pizza parlors. These mathematical madmen had come up with an ingenious way to figure out how much dough the pizza parlors were making so they could have their slice of the pie. The IRS calculated the standard amount of flour in a pizza, divided that number by the total amount of flour purchased by the restaurant, compared that to the actual number of pizzas made, and then determined the projected income of the store. If their figure was more than the figure the pizza parlor was reporting, the store had to deliver the extra taxes to the IRS.

pizza

P politicians

Democrat Michael Heagerty worked for weeks to get enough signatures on his petition to run for reelection to the city council in Syracuse, New York, but missed the required number by one vote (he was credited with 334 of the 335 signatures necessary). According to an August 11, 2009, article in the *Syracuse Post-Standard*, Heagerty realized too late that he had forgotten to sign his own petition but stated he would run for reelection anyway but as an independent.

STUPID

"Any person who shall not lift his hat to the mayor as he passes him on the street will be guilty of a misdemeanor."

—COLUMBUS, MONTANA, ORDINANCE

S tu Rasmussen was elected mayor of Silverton, Oregon, in 2008 even though he openly dresses as a woman. According to a July 23, 2009, report from Portland television station KATU-TV, Rasmussen was criticized by officials of a community group after addressing students while wearing a miniskirt and a swimsuit top. The criticism wasn't that he wore women's clothes but that he should have worn "professional" women's clothes when speaking to the youth group.

T he *Miami Herald* reported on March 11, 2009, that during a Florida Senate debate on whether to exempt "animal husbandry" from the law against bestiality, state senator Larcenia Bullard asked in earnest, "People are taking these animals as husbands?"

"Nothing is more important in the face of a war than cutting taxes."

—TOM DELAY (R-TX), SPEAKING AT AN AMERICA'S COMMUNITY BANKERS MEETING, MARCH 12, 2003

After reading to a room full of fourth graders at Jo Mackey Elementary School, on March 2, 2005, Oscar Goodman, the mayor of Las Vegas, was asked by one wide-eyed youth what his hobbies were. "Drinking" was one the mayor mentioned. Another child asked the mayor what one thing he would want if he were stranded on a deserted island. "A bottle of gin," the mayor replied.

Goodman was neither shaken nor stirred about the ensuing controversy and stated, "I'm the George Washington of mayors. I can't tell a lie." During a press conference at city hall the following day, the mayor was asked if he thought he had a drinking problem. Goodman said, "Absolutely not. No. I love to drink." See? No problem.

It is a federal law that no one can throw tomatoes or eggs, rotten or not, at a member of Congress while such member is making a speech or campaigning for office. The maximum sentence for pummeling a congressperson is one year in prison and a $5,000 fine.

Brunswick, Maine, District 1 town councilor David Watson resigned from his position as council vice chairman on January 23, 2007, after unintentionally forwarding an e-mail to eighteen members of the New Elementary School Building Committee. The e-mail contained nine embedded images of topless women under the heading "This is National Women's Breast Awareness Day." The only other text in the e-mail read, "Beats . . . Martin Luther King Day, doesn't it?" I bet he felt like a real boob after that.

praying

If you're too busy to pray then the Web site InformationAgePrayer.com has the answer. The site offers a personalized daily invocation for the God and religion of your choice: Catholic, Protestant, Jewish, or Muslim. A voice-synthesized software can recite the Lord's Prayer or the Islamic Fajr for $3.95 a month. For the Catholics, there's a choice of Hail Marys for $0.70 a day for a set of ten. A complete rosary package is $49.95 a month according to a March 25, 2009, report from LiveScience.com. Just so God knows who the prayer is from, the computer screen displays your name and, in the case of a prayer to Allah, the Web site's speakers are faced toward Mecca.

On May 23, 2009, the *Charlotte Observer* ran a story about David Cerullo, who achieved some prominence after purchasing the television studios abandoned by Jim and Tammy Faye Bakker's PTL Club. Along with his father, semi-retired Pentecostal preacher Morris Cerullo, they formed the Inspiration Network, which touts a "prosperity gospel" ministry. David, who receives an annual base salary of $1.52 million (his wife and children are also on the payroll) assures followers that the more they give (to them) the more God will give in return. The newspaper reported on the Cerullos' most recent television commercial in which Morris, first speaking in tongues, addresses his currently credit-challenged flock with "When you [donate], the windows of heaven . . . open for you . . . 100 fold." Meanwhile, an on-screen message flashes: "Call now with your $900 offering and receive God's debt cancellation!"

Baltimore prosecutors charged forty-year-old cult leader "Queen Antoinette" of the 1 Mind Ministries with the starvation death of a sixteen-month-old boy who refused to say "Amen" at meal times. Their case was thwarted, however, when the boy's mother, cult member Ria Ramkissoon, refused to file charges against the Queen, ultimately believing that she would bring her dead son back to life.

According to a March 31, 2009, article in the *Washington Post*, the judge in the case announced that an agreement had been made in which Ramkissoon would cooperate if prosecutors would promise, in writing, that all charges against the Queen would be dropped if she actually brought the boy back from the dead.

presidents

While researching his family history for a reunion in his hometown of Plains, Georgia, Jimmy Carter came to this conclusion: "Sometimes it's good not to know too much about your own family." Carter uncovered, among other things, that his great-great-grandfather, Wiley Carter, killed a man for stealing a slave. Carter's great-grandfather was shot to death in a gunfight in 1873 by his business partner. And in 1903, Carter's grandfather died after being shot in the back by a man who stole a table from the family store. "As far as I know," Carter said, "most of the other family members have been both law-abiding and peaceful in nature." Well, not quite: Let's not forget Billy!

Valentine's Day, 1914, was the worst day in Theodore Roosevelt's life: His mother died of typhoid fever in the morning, and in the afternoon, his wife died giving birth to their daughter.

P

John Tyler wasn't honored by his country after his death on January 18, 1862, and no official word of his death was ever issued. Why? Because Tyler was considered a traitor in the North even though he had been president of the United States. On May 5, 1861, Tyler accepted a seat in the provisional congress of the Confederate States of America. A few months later he was elected to represent his congressional district in the permanent CSA Congress. Tyler was truly a Rebel and the only U.S. president to ever hold office in the Confederacy. When he died he even had a Confederate flag, not an American flag, draped over his casket. It wasn't until fifty years after the Civil War ended, in 1915, that the United States finally erected a memorial stone over his grave.

Thomas Jefferson and James Madison were both arrested in Vermont in the spring of 1791 for the crime of carriage riding on a Sunday.

A few of the things we associate with George Washington: He chopped down the cherry tree (which he didn't), he threw a silver dollar across the Potomac River (which he didn't; silver dollars weren't minted until four years before Washington's death—and besides, it would take a cannon to shoot a coin across the wide banks of the Potomac), and his dentures were made out of wood—which also isn't true. Washington's dentures were, in fact, made out of hippopotamus ivory. A New York City dentist, John Greenwood, made President Washington several sets of dentures. Greenwood tried for years to save the last remaining tooth Washington had (the first bicuspid in his left lower jaw). In 1789, Greenwood made Washington's first set of dentures out of human teeth (not Washington's) fastened with gold rivets with the remainder made of hippo ivory.

Sadly, Greenwood had to extract the president's last remaining tooth in 1796 and had it encased in a gold locket and inscribed: "In New York 1790. Jn Greenwood made Pres Geo Washington a whole sett of teeth. The enclosed tooth is the last one which grew in his head." Wow, some people will keep anything.

presidents

"I don't necessarily consider McDonald's junk food. You know, they have chicken sandwiches, they have salads."

—Bill Clinton in 1993, defending his favorite fast food chain

prisoners

Soon after being made a jail trusty, inmate Ross Chadwell tried to escape the Benton County, Arkansas, prison where he was incarcerated. He was soon captured and punished for his actions. He then filed a lawsuit against both the county and Sheriff Andy Lee claiming civil rights violations. Chadwell accused Sheriff Lee of acting "recklessly" by making him a trusty and therefore putting him in a position that made it possible for him to attempt escape.

Ernesto Mota filed a $7 million lawsuit in 1993 claiming the police in Oak Forest, Illinois, acted negligently after his arrest. Mota swallowed a bag of cocaine, which was to be used as evidence against him, and subsequently suffered severe brain damage. He alleged the police should have stopped him, or at least helped him receive medical attention more quickly.

According to an April 17, 2002, Associated Press article, a prisoner in a Kingman, Arizona, jail accidentally died after he excreted on the floor of his cell and then later slipped on it and cracked his head.

Amil Dinsio, a federal prisoner in Loretto, Pennsylvania, filed a $15 million lawsuit against the United Carolina Bank in Charlotte, North Carolina. Dinsio, who robbed the bank in 1992, was sentenced according to the amount of money he stole. Dinsio claims the bank exaggerated the amount, which resulted in an additional sixteen months to his sentence.

P

An inmate serving time in a Genoa, Italy, jail escaped during a work program and left without a trace. Well, not exactly without a trace. The fleeing felon accidentally dropped his wallet while on the run and the police confiscated it. Inside the wallet was the criminal's cellular telephone number. Acting on a hunch (a hunch that the escaped prisoner was stupid) the police called the number and told the escapee he could pick up his lost wallet at police headquarters. Several hours later the convict arrived at the station on a stolen moped to collect the wallet. Instead he was collected by the police and charged with evading jail and theft. It seems the man's cell phone had a clear signal but his connection with reality was fuzzy.

P

prisoners

Merrill Chamberlain, who is serving a life sentence for the shooting death of an Albuquerque, New Mexico, police officer, had his lawsuit dismissed by the U.S. Court of Appeals in Denver. Chamberlain claimed the police officer wouldn't have died had the officer been wearing a bulletproof vest.

Jose Rivera Martinez, an inmate in Schenectady, New York, filed a $750,000 lawsuit in February 1993 against the county jail claiming he was allergic to the jail-issued hot dogs. His lawsuit alleged that the hot dogs he was forced to eat made him develop warts, which permanently disfigured him.

psychiatry

Roger Chamberlain was arrested in Binghamton, New York, according to a May 17, 2004, article in *Newsday*, for allegedly smearing fourteen jars' worth of petroleum jelly on nearly every inch of the walls and furniture of a Motel 6 room. Chamberlain was later discovered staying at another motel; this time he himself was covered in the slippery substance.

"PSYCHOPATHS COULD BE BEST FINANCIAL TRADERS—RESEARCH"

—REUTERS HEADLINE, SEPTEMBER 19, 2005

A woman who told Roswell, New Mexico, police she had been on another planet for three years reported a robbery, according to a May 29, 2001, article in the *Roswell Daily Record*. She said someone had taken the upper plate of her dentures valued at $800, silverware valued at $1,000, and $1,000 in jewelry. She said she hadn't actually seen the named suspect take the items, because he "moves so swift you can't see him."

P **S** teven McDonald served as his own lawyer during his arson trial in Mount Vernon, Washington, and while he was cross-examining himself he would pose the question as McDonald the lawyer and then answer as McDonald the accused arsonist. According to the February 7, 2002, article in the *Skagit Valley Herald*, in order to refute earlier testimony from a key police witness who had stated that McDonald was seen at the crime scene "arguing with himself," McDonald knew he needed to directly question himself.

"Mr. McDonald," McDonald the lawyer asked. "Have you ever talked to yourself?"

Escaped from the
Montana State Hospital for the
mentally ill in Warm Springs:
Mr. Terry Crazy.

—ASSOCIATED PRESS, MAY 26, 2001

We've all heard that fish is brain food, but one Cape Town, South African man could do well eating more fish as opposed to throwing them. The *Cape Times* ran a story on November 21, 2002, about the man's odd habit of throwing rotten fish at people: people in their cars, train passengers, and even congregants of a local church. Police didn't arrested the man as his activities weren't considered serious, and they hoped he would voluntarily scale back on his fish-flinging fetish.

An emergency call was received about an apartment fire in June 2000 in Fargo, North Dakota, and firefighters and police were dispatched. Upon arriving at the apartment, emergency personal encountered thick smoke billowing from a window and a stench that one crewmember described as "noxious and terrible." After the door was broken down firefighters noticed the tenant standing in a corner with his fists raised as if to fight. The man eventually revealed both the cause and the source of the fire: He routinely collects all his cut hair from barber visits and once a year piles it all in a pan and sets it on fire. The man claimed he worked for the FBI and was arrested for threatening the firefighters.

P

According to a July 9, 2003, article in the *Vancouver Sun*, an inmate at a psychiatric prison in Abbotsford, British Columbia, flew into a fierce frenzy and took his therapist hostage after fellow inmates made fun of his drawing of "toilet paper" during a game of Pictionary.

"He becomes aroused by females sneezing . . . In my entire career I've never heard of anything like this," said police chief Kerry Crews of Commerce, Texas. He was talking about a man who was arrested after twice approaching a female clerk at Commerce Hardware and, according to a September 25, 2009, article in the *Greenville Herald Banner*, held up a piece of paper with powder on it and blew it into her face to cause her to sneeze.

FOX News reported on May 8, 2009, that specialists from the New York State Psychiatric Institute are in the middle of a two-year investigation that nightly takes them into gay bars in Buenos Aires where they question men about their sexual behavior and their drug use. The researchers are working from a $400,000 grant from the National Institutes of Health to study why gay men have risky sex in Argentina.

Thirty-three-year-old Wendy Brown, who has a history of identify-theft issues, enrolled at Ashwaubenon High School in Green Bay, Wisconsin, pretending to be her fifteen-year-old daughter (who actually lives in Nevada). According to a September 12, 2008, article in the *Wisconsin State Journal*, one theory as to why Brown enrolled herself is that she is acting out a longtime fantasy of becoming a cheerleader. Brown regularly attended practices and had actually made the squad when she was arrested for identify theft.

Neighbors in a Mesa, Arizona, apartment complex called police to report a fight between a man and a woman that involved screaming and objects being broken. According to a July 1, 2008, article in the *Arizona Republic*, police, including SWAT, arrived at the scene only to find a twenty-one-year-old man was solely responsible for the argument. Apparently the man changed his voice from that of a woman to that of a man in order to argue with himself. He was taken in for a medical exam.

P

psychiatry

Stephen Peterson returned to court in Sydney, Australia, ten years after his original trial to challenge the "not guilty/insanity" decision that was ruled against him. Peterson argued that he should have been allowed to call as defense witnesses a number of "higher beings," who had been responsible in urging him to kill. According to the *Fairfax Media*, an Auckland, New Zealand, newspaper, Peterson pleaded with the court to call to his defense "Spacedust" the "sun god" and "Kadec" the "plasma being." The court turned down his request.

On August 22, 2007, the *Daily Mail* reported that British physician Stuart Brown had been arrested for beating his wife and was released after paying only a small fine. In his defense Brown explained that the fight was caused after he lost control because a "red mist" had descended on the room.

questionable | Q

Jessica Cohen of Cincinnati, Ohio, went to the local public defender's office seeking a lawyer to represent her on a theft charge. According to a November 3, 2008, article in the *Cincinnati Enquirer*, Cohen filled out paperwork, which included her name and address, and then stole an employee's cell phone. She was later rearrested on charges of theft.

Merle Sorenson felt he needed to clean the tires on his Humvee and wanted to see how far he could drive his vehicle into the Columbia River near Quincy, Washington, and still be able to back out. According to an October 31, 2008, article in the *Seattle Times*, he had to be rescued after nearly drowning when the Humvee was swept downstream.

Sharon Platt allegedly stole approximately $5,000 from her employer, Murphy Motors of Williston, North Dakota, and left town, according to a May 23, 2008, article in the *Grand Forks Herald*. She resettled in Pittsburgh, Pennsylvania, and decided to apply for a job. In the job application she listed Murphy Motors as a reference. When the human resources department called her former employer, he alerted Pittsburgh police.

Police in Redding, California, were chasing two men who had been trying to break into Northern California Recycling and then set out on foot through a residential neighborhood. One suspect was quickly apprehended, but the other one eluded capture—despite the fact that six police officers, a helicopter, and a police dog were chasing him. Police issued a report that the man was wearing khaki pants and a San Francisco 49ers logo sweatshirt, and that gave Russell Spade, who was living in the neighborhood and listening to his police scanner, an idea.

Spade put on a pair of khaki pants and a 49ers sweatshirt and went outside to see if officers "noticed" him. "Well, we noticed him," said Sergeant Steve Moravec. According to a November 17, 2009, article in the *Redding Record Searchlight*, police quickly determined that Spade wasn't the man they were looking for (as he didn't fit the rest of the suspect's description), but they arrested him anyway for obstructing and delaying a police officer.

Q

questionable

queens

No matter what the revisionists say, Cleopatra was not black—she wasn't even Egyptian. The Cleopatra I'm talking about, the one Elizabeth Taylor portrayed, was actually titled Cleopatra VII Thea Philopator (there were seven queens named Cleopatra). Cleo was part Greek, part Macedonian, and part Iranian. She ruled Egypt from Alexandria, which, other than its location, was not an Egyptian city at all. It would be like someone in the future deciding the prime minister of South Africa in the 1980s and '90s was black because South Africa is part of Africa and Africans are dark-skinned—not taking into account that South Africa was part of Great Britain and therefore the county's leaders were British. Now we know Cleopatra wasn't black— and you can bet she didn't look like Elizabeth Taylor, either.

Because she is a member of the royal family and not a commoner, the queen of England is not allowed to enter the House of Commons.

In 1939, during a trip across Canada, King George VI and his wife, Queen Elizabeth, were greeted by Canadian prime minister William Lyon MacKenzie King. The mayor of Winnipeg and his wife—Mr. and Mrs. John Queen, also greeted them. So in a bizarre, but true, variation of Abbott and Costello's famous "Who's on First" routine, here is a partial transcript from the Canadian Broadcasting Corporation's announcement of the event:

"Here comes the royal family now. The automobile has now stopped, a member of the RCMP is opening the car door— oh, there's the king—he's stepping out, followed by Her Majesty Queen Elizabeth, nattily attired in a silver coat.

"Mr. King is now shaking hands with the king and introducing Mr. Queen to the king and queen and then Mrs. Queen to the queen and king. They are now proceeding up the steps to the well-decorated city hall, the king and Mr. King together, with the queen being escorted by Mrs. Queen. The king has now stopped and said something to Mrs. Queen, . . . and the queen and Mr. King laughed jovially. The king leaves Mr. King and goes to Mrs. Queen, and the queen and Mr. King follow behind."

quotations

"[They were] two kids who had nothing better to do. They don't have cable TV— what do you do?"

—Defense lawyer Paul Fernadex, citing a possible reason, in a Paterson, New Jersey, court in March 1994, as to why his client, a fourteen-year-old boy, might have sexually assaulted an eleven-year-old girl

"I should have blown your f— king head off! If I'd been the one that was there."

—Dennis Newton, in an Oklahoma City courtroom in 1985, reacting to a witness who identified him as the person who held up a gas station

"I'm sellin' dope / And I was gettin' paid / Too blind to see / How I was gettin' played."

—ERIC CLARK, THEN TWENTY-TWO, RAPPING A PLEA TO THE JUDGE FOR A LIGHT SENTENCE IN DECEMBER 1994. HE RECEIVED TWENTY-THREE YEARS IN PRISON.

"We aren't criminals. If we had gotten away with it, it would never have happened again."

—A TWENTY-ONE-YEAR-OLD MAN ACCUSED, ALONG WITH HIS PARTNER, OF BEATING A WOMAN TO DEATH AND THEN RUNNING OVER HER WITH A CAR

"A lot of kids fantasize about me. I have monster trucks and boats and stuff."

—A FORTY-FOUR-YEAR-OLD MAN ACQUITTED OF SODOMY WITH A TWELVE-YEAR-OLD GIRL BY A FLORENCE, ALABAMA, JURY IN JUNE OF 1992, EXPLAINING WHY THE CHILD MIGHT HAVE MADE UP THE STORY ABOUT HIM

racism

According to an article in the *Chicago Sun-Times*, a University of Pennsylvania student group, White Women Against Racism, excluded a black woman who expressed an interest in joining the group. A spokesperson for the group explained that whites have to meet among fellow whites in order to understand why they so often exclude blacks. "[R]acism is a white problem, and we have a responsibility as white women in particular to do what we can to eradicate racism."

The Walworth County, Wisconsin, Board of Supervisors drafted an anti-bigotry resolution changing a reference to white supremacist organizations from "hate groups" to "unhappy groups."

In 1983, Theresa Mulqueen Skeeter, a light-skinned black woman, sued her employer, a municipal agency located in Norfolk, Virginia, for racial discrimination. She claimed she was discriminated against because she was black, stating that she was born and raised black and brought up in the company of black relatives. Four years later, she filed a similar complaint against the same agency, this time charging racial discrimination against her because she looks white.

The Harvard Divinity School, in a "Green Earth" policy, placed recycling bins around campus to collect paper. The bins were originally labeled "white" and "colored." An anonymous prankster relabeled the "colored" bin to read "paper of color." To which school officials relabeled both bins as "bleached paper" and "dyed paper."

R

An article in the *Fresno Bee* concerning the Massachusetts budget crisis had obviously been run through the "politically correct spell checker" as it referred to new taxes that could put the state "back in the African-American."

A small metal-forming shop in Chicago was cited by the Equal Employment Opportunity Commission for hiring too many Hispanic and Polish-American workers and no blacks. The EEOC forced the company to run an advertisement inviting blacks to file claims for compensation on the basis of discrimination. One hundred and twenty-seven were awarded payouts—even if they had never applied for a job at that company.

Boston Latin High School now refers to Chinese New Year's Day as "Asian New Year's," regardless of the fact that other Asian cultures celebrate the New Year on different days.

relationships

A s Anthony Miller was robbing a bank in Ephrata, Pennsylvania, he continued to ask the teller the same question. It wasn't "Have you filled the bag with cash yet?"—it was "Did you call the police yet?" During Miller's sentencing, after it was disclosed that he had used a BB gun during the robbery, Miller admitted he wanted to go to prison because he wanted to get away from his wife.

"I was scared," he told Judge Louis Farina. "She was very abusive to me." According to a September 2, 2009, Associated Press article, Robert Beyer, who represented Miller, told the judge that when a police officer interviewed Miller's wife, he said that after twenty minutes "I was ready for jail, too." Judge Farina sentenced Miller to three to six years in prison.

relationships

An October 2, 2008, article in *Florida Today* reported that after Jonathon Guabello and his girlfriend arrived home from a bar, he became angry when she denied him sex. Police in Fort Myers, Florida, said Guabello stormed out of the room, took a pistol, and shot himself in the arm, twice. He lost his balance because of the pain, hit his head on the kitchen stove, and knocked himself unconscious. After he regained consciousness, Guabello was arrested for domestic assault and firing a weapon in an occupied dwelling.

A twenty-five-year-old woman was arrested for assault in Bremerton, Washington, for punching her boyfriend in the face several times, causing him to slip in the shower and dislocate his shoulder. According to a December 28, 2007, Associated Press article, the fight started after the man asked if his dog could join them in the shower. When she refused, the boyfriend said he hoped his next girlfriend would be more understanding of his dog—and that's when she threw the first punch.

religion R

The Church of Spiritual Humanism was investigated by the village of Lake Bluff, Illinois, because it claimed a religious exemption from property tax. It turns out that the church building is actually the home of the church's founder and millionaire Chicago banker George Michael. During the investigation it was discovered that the photograph Michael included with his tax application had the cross "drawn on [it] with a marker and did not physically exist at the time the photo was taken." As reported by ABC News, the county sent Michael a property tax bill of $225,000 for 2007 through 2009.

An FBI sex sting in St. Louis, Missouri, caught James Patrick Grady when he arrived to have sex with a person he believed to be a sixteen-year-old girl. He confessed to his actions and later told prosecutors that his employer had agreed to pay for a defense attorney and bail him out of jail on the condition that he be released before trial. Grady is an employee of the Roman Catholic Church—a priest at St. Raphael the Archangel. According to a report by KSDK-TV on June 24, 2010, Grady was later caught with child pornography on his computer and was subsequently sentenced to nearly seven years in prison.

"**D**on't call, take it easy, they said they will let me go," read the text sent by Wikler Moran-Mora to his wife. The thirty-eight-year-old Tampa, Florida, resident claimed that he had been kidnapped, and when his wife said she was calling police he quickly replied that he had been let go. The Hillsborough County Sheriff's Office tracked his phone call to a 7-Eleven and discovered Moran-Mora, a pastor at the Seventh Day Adventist Church of Reform, had faked the incident as cover, as he was spending time with his girlfriend, a sheriff's spokesman said. According to an August 27, 2009, article in the *Tampa Tribune*, he was charged with making a false report and released on a $500 bond.

Pastor Jeff Harlow of Crossroads Community Church in Kokomo, Indiana, wanted to illustrate a sermon on "unity" by drawing the analogy of "being one" with a dirt bike. According to a July 22, 2008, Associated Press article, "Harley Harlow" drove the bike off the stage and into the empty front row, breaking his wrist, cutting his head, and garnering several bruises (including one to his ego).

R

Lauren M. Hanley was arrested for drunken driving after she was involved in a single-car accident at Wantagh, New York, in which she crashed into a tree. Hanley admitted she had consumed half of the bottle of gin police discovered in her car, and her blood-alcohol level was more than twice the legal limit. According to a September 3, 2009, article in *Newsday*, Sister Hanley, a nun, was driving a church-owned vehicle and was on her way to work at the St. Frances de Chantal Church.

Based on the story found in John 13:1–17 in the Bible, Pastor Bob Book and his wife wash the feet of three dozen homeless men every Monday at their Church of the Common Ground in Atlanta, Georgia. But this is not a simple soak and rinse; these pedicures include a massage, pumice rubbing, nail trimming, and a free pair of clean socks. According to a January 22, 2009, Associated Press article, Book claims that "worst ongoing" threat to the homeless and others isn't the influence of Satan but foot fungus. "It eats away and destroys the toenails and just makes it very hard for people to walk," Book said.

religion

On November 19, 2008, the *Local*, a Swedish newspaper, reported that artist Carlos Bebeacua was allowed to register the Madonna of Orgasm Church as a legitimate place of worship.

The *Bristol Herald Courier* reported on July 31, 2007, that the minister of the Gospel Baptist Church in Bristol, Virginia, fifty-eight-year-old Tommy Tester, was arrested in an alcohol-related incident. Apparently Tester was allegedly seen urinating at a car wash, in front of both children and police officers, while wearing a skirt.

religion

According to an August 27, 2007, article in the *Atlanta Journal-Constitution*, televangelist Bishop Thomas Weeks III was arrested for allegedly beating up and threatening to kill his estranged wife, televangelist Juanita Bynum. The fight occurred in a hotel parking lot, and Bynum was rescued by a bellman before any harm could come to her. Weeks blamed the incident on Satan. Not surprisingly, the two were soon divorced and on October 17, 2009, Weeks married Prophetess Christina Glenn, whom he had found through his online reality TV show called *The Next Mrs. Weeks*.

Pastor Walter Steen of Detroit, Michigan, pleaded guilty to tax fraud and was sentenced to fifteen months in prison. Steen worked at H&R Block in 2001 and at Jackson Hewitt from 2002 to 2004, and then started his own tax business, God Will Provide Tax Service, in 2005. According to an August 2, 2007, article in the *Detroit News*, out of the 1,578 returns he prepared for clients, 1,573 claimed tax refunds.

reptiles

A 114-pound tortoise, part of the Zambini Family Circus performing in Madison, Wisconsin, escaped according to a July 18, 2009, Associated Press article. The tortoise actually made good time on his race for freedom, covering a hair over two miles in six days before being recaptured.

Horned toads are not toads—they are lizards.

R

reptiles

Portland, Oregon, police and firefighters were dispatched by a 911 call to check on a five-year-old boy who had been attacked by an animal. These calls can be quite an ordeal: a crying, bleeding child; an animal that has to be hunted down and possibly destroyed; frightened parents. When fireman Hal Westberg arrived on the scene, he realized the situation wasn't as dramatic as all that. A young boy had stuck his tongue out at his pet turtle, who responded by chomping down on the boy's tongue and not letting go. The turtle stayed latched on for fifteen minutes until officials showed up. Westberg said he simply slipped his pen in the turtle's mouth, added a little pressure, and the turtle let go. The young boy didn't require medical attention. As for the turtle—he was transferred to a minimum-security tank at a relative's house.

In Michigan, you are not allowed to tie your pet crocodile to a fire hydrant.

An eight-year-old boy from University Place, Washington, found out the hard way why his pet turtle is called a box turtle. The boy was poking at the turtle when Boxer clamped down on his finger and wouldn't let go. A 911 call dispatched firefighters, who arrived to find the turtle still firmly attached. They tried offering the turtle food and tapping on his shell to get him to let go. Then they thought of using nitrous oxide, commonly known as laughing gas.

"We just blew a little in his face, he relaxed, and the kid pulled his finger out," said paramedic Steve Murphy. The boy was relieved and suffered only a blood blister on his finger. Firefighters reported that Boxer was "totally stoned" but would peacefully sleep it off. "That's why they're called box turtles," said veterinarian Darrell Kraft who specializes in turtles. "They can close up tight just like a box."

The city of Toledo, Ohio, has made it illegal to throw any type of reptile at another person.

reptiles

In order to get close enough to enormous Nile crocodiles to attach data monitors to their tails, Dr. Brady Barr, a reptile specialist with the National Geographic TV channel, donned a crocodile suit and crawled to them. Barr, who also smeared hippopotamus dung on himself to mask his human scent, approached the twenty-foot-long reptiles in Tanzania and began tagging them as part of his research. The *Daily Mirror* reported on Barr's activities in an article from June 13, 2007, and wrote that the scariest moment didn't involve the crocodiles but a curious hippopotamus who was attracted by the smell of the dung.

The blindworm, also known as the slowworm or deaf adder, is neither blind nor deaf nor even slow—heck, it isn't even a worm or an adder. The blindworm is actually a legless lizard that can see, hear, and move as quickly as a normal snake.

research

Tonda Hughes of the University of Illinois at Chicago, the lead researcher on a $3 million grant from the National Institutes of Health, is delving into the issue of why lesbians drink alcohol. According to a July 21, 2009, article in the *Chicago Sun-Times*, Hughes wants to compare why lesbians drink with why heterosexual women drink.

Duke Medical Center researchers announced in an August 22, 2007, article in *Nature* that they had achieved success engineering mice with obsessive-compulsive disorder.

According to a July 12, 2009, article in the *Daily Telegraph*, psychology researchers at Britain's Keele University proved that, in response to danger, people who curse are better able to endure pain than those who use milder language.

"RESEARCHER LINKS OBESITY, FOOD PORTIONS"

—ASSOCIATED PRESS HEADLINE, JANUARY 3, 2004

Researchers from Wayne State University in Detroit, Michigan, are working from a $2.6 million National Institutes of Health grant to "train" prostitutes to drink alcohol responsibly. According to a May 14, 2009, FOX News report, the training is intended to reduce a prostitute's willingness to engage in risky or unprotected sex. The Detroit researchers are dealing with prostitutes working in the Guangxi Province in China.

"ALLEGATIONS OF FAKE RESEARCH HIT NEW HIGH"

—ASSOCIATED PRESS HEADLINE, JULY 12, 2005

research

B ritish scientists were honored with the 2002 Ig Nobel award for their research into the reproductive habits of the ostrich. Their observations uncovered that ostriches become more sexually aroused when there was a human present—in fact, some ostriches tried to become amorous with the human observers.

"LARGER KANGAROOS LEAP FARTHER, RESEARCHERS FIND"

—LOS ANGELES TIMES HEADLINE, NOVEMBER 2, 1995

A n article in the May 21, 2007, issue of *New Scientist* reported that Argentinean researchers have discovered that hamsters fed the erectile dysfunction drug Viagra were able to endure the rigors of jet lag nearly 50 percent better than hamsters fed a placebo.

R retribution

On March 10, 2008, the *Salt Lake Tribune* reported that a thirty-one-year-old man was transported to a local hospital in critical condition after he jumped out of a cab in order to avoid paying the fee. Before he got too far an oncoming car struck him.

After trying to run down his girlfriend with his car, a twenty-five-year-old man was chased by police when he fled on foot. According to a February 15, 2008, article in the *Houston Chronicle*, the man was running across Interstate 45 when he was struck and killed by several cars.

According to a March 30, 2008, article in the *St. Petersburg Times*, two men who stole a kayak and went joyriding on Moon Lake near New Port Richey, Florida, drowned when the boat capsized.

revenge

An unidentified man in Panama City, Florida, took one look at Amanda Hicks's baby and did the dumbest thing in his life—he made fun of the way the child looked. According to a December 25, 2002, article in the *Panama City News Herald*, the twenty-year-old mom and two of her girlfriends jumped into action and punched, kicked, kneed, stripped, and burned the man and then sodomized him with two different objects.

revenge

Snohomish County, Washington, deputy prosecutor Valerie Shapiro said a seventy-eight-year-old Lynnwood woman (whose name was not released) admitted to repeatedly beating her eighty-four-year-old husband and turned over her diary to prove it. "I beat him again," read one entry after the woman was arrested for kicking her husband in the groin, hitting him with a pipe, and smashing him over the head with a bowl. "I told him it would be worth going to jail just to watch him bleed to death."

The entry goes on to describe her feelings after she attacked her husband with a carpet sweeper and a knife. According to a May 19, 2009, article in the *Everett Herald*, the woman was still seeking revenge for an alleged affair her husband had—thirty-five years ago.

Nearly one hundred cats died in an early morning fire at a humane society shelter in Oshawa, Ontario, according to a December 19, 2008, article in the *Toronto Star*. The fire marshal's office confirmed that the inferno was probably the result of mice chewing through electrical wires.

The New Zealand Press Association released a story on October 8, 2008, about a twenty-one-year-old woman who was arrested in Hamilton, New Zealand, for assault after she allegedly kicked in the door of her ex-boyfriend's home, then attacked him over a custody dispute involving their pet possum.

After making noise complaints about his upstairs neighbors, forty-three-year-old Christopher Sullivan of Oshkosh, Wisconsin, sent them threatening packages, according to an August 26, 2008, article in the *Northwestern*. One of the packages contained a Polaroid photo of three naked Barbie dolls with their heads removed. When Sullivan was arrested he admitted he was angry with his neighbors because they made too much noise when they were having sex.

R

revenge

Novelist Krystian Bala of Warsaw, Poland, was arrested in 2007 for the torture and murder of a businessman in 2000. Bala might have gotten away with the murder except that he couldn't resist writing about it in his debut 2003 novel, *Amok*. An anonymous source tipped off investigators to the similarities in the book to the actual murder with details that could only have been known by the killer. According to an August 9, 2007, article in the *Times*, further investigation tied Bala to the crime, including the fact that the victim was Bala's ex-wife's lover. He was sentenced to twenty-five years in prison.

science S

Scientists at the Institute for Animal Health in Edinburgh secured a £217,000 government grant and spent five years trying to discover whether bovine spongiform encephalopathy (commonly referred to as "mad cow disease") had crossed the "species barrier" from cows into sheep. In October 2001 the program was investigated after it was discovered that scientists had inadvertently been testing cattle brains instead of sheep brains for the entire five years.

The Avery Coonley School in Illinois was banned for two years from the state science fair. Had the school been caught cheating, or were students engaging in illegal activities? Nope, they were barred from the fair because they had won the championship four years in a row and officials wanted to give other schools a chance to win the title for a change.

S

science

Finally, science has tackled the age-old problem of when an egg has been properly boiled soft, medium, or hard. The *Times* reported on July 31, 2006, that the British Egg Information Service (I'm not joking) announced the perfection and availability of the "smart egg." Throw that old egg timer away; the new "smart egg" has an invisible ink on the shell that turns black at the moment of your boiled preference.

As part of an experiment to study the effects and causes of landslides, Japanese scientists in 1971 watered down a hill using fire hoses to simulate the effect of a torrential rainstorm. The soil on the hill gave way and the resulting landslide killed four scientists and eleven observers.

seat belts

Working under a grant, police in West Hazleton, Pennsylvania, set up special patrols under the "Buckle Up" program designed to enforce the state's seat belt law. Police noticed a car traveling at a high rate of speed and erratically changing lanes without use of a turn signal. When they stopped the car, officers noticed a glass bong in plain sight on the passenger's seat and arrested Ryan Neaus. In his defense, Neaus explained to the officers that he was speeding "because he was chasing the person who just robbed him of his Apple iPhone and three bags of marijuana," the resulting report says. A subsequent search of the vehicle revealed fifteen baggies of marijuana and thirteen ecstasy pills. According to a June 8, 2009, article in the *Wilkes Barre Times Leader*, Neaus was arrested on drug charges as well as failure to wear a seat belt.

S

seat belts

Thirty-nine-year-old Ivan Segedin, of Okato, New Zealand, had been cited thirty-two times for driving without a seat belt. Segedin, to give the illusion to passing motorists and police officers, had rigged a fake belt in his car that simply sat over his shoulder. According to a February 23, 2008, article in the *Fairfax News*, Segedin was thrown against the steering wheel of his car and died when he was involved in a low-impact crash. Coroner Carla na Nagara said not wearing the seat belt was the one variable that made the difference between life and death for Segedin.

seat belts

"The rear half of the car was cut right off and stayed under the pole," a police spokesman from Blacktown, New South Wales, in Australia, said, "and the front portion skidded and jumped for another seventy-two feet before it stopped with the driver still in it." Rescue crews called to the scene of the January 2003 accident found the seventeen-year-old driver, strapped in his seat belt, virtually unharmed and still fighting with his girlfriend on his cell phone. According to an article in the *Surry Hills Daily Telegraph*, the driver was having an argument with his girlfriend when he hit a pole going approximately 94 mph.

The *Sydney Morning Herald* reported on a family of three who was injured in a car crash because the mother was too drunk to drive. But she really didn't cause the accident because although she was behind the wheel she let someone else steer—her five-year-old son. The car careened off the Bli Bli Road on the Sunshine Coast in Australia, hit a tree, hurtled down an embankment, and came to rest in an enclosed field. No one in the car was wearing seat belts; all were thrown from their vehicle and suffered minor injuries after the January 2008 accident.

S

seat belts

Mary Ubaudi of Madison County, Illinois, was a passenger in a car driven by William Humphrey when, she claimed, he started driving too fast, lost control of the car in a construction zone, and flipped it over. She was thrown from the vehicle and sustained severe and life-threatening injuries. So Ubaudi sued Humphrey—no big deal, right? Well, it wouldn't be interesting enough for this book except that Ubaudi didn't just sue Humphrey for "at least $50,000"; she's also suing Rowe Construction for "at least $50,000" and Mazda Motors, the manufacturer of Humphrey's Miata, for "in excess of $150,000." According to a November 2004 article in the *Madison County Record*, Ubaudi's lawsuit claims the car manufacturer "failed to provide instructions regarding the safe and proper use of a seat belt."

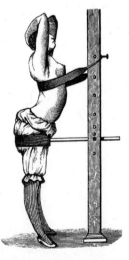

Palm Bay, Florida, patrol officer Jason McCoy stopped a driver for failure to wear a seat belt in accordance with the state's new seat belt law. But when he pulled the car over, the driver jumped out of the vehicle, allegedly with a bag of cocaine in his hands, and tried to run. McCoy warned the suspect, Travis Lee Brown, to stop, and eventually had to subdue him with a Taser. Further investigation revealed Brown was in possession of approximately eight grams of cocaine and thirteen Oxycodone pills. Brown was taken to the Palm Bay Police Department for processing, at which time he became "irate" about not being able to make a phone call.

While in the holding cell, Brown began to do a handstand and, according to Officer McCoy, "acted like he passed out." Brown was wanted by Richmond County, Georgia, authorities on charges related to kidnapping and carjacking, according to a July 1, 2009, Palm Bay Police Department news release.

S

sex

You can't have sex with a virgin in the state of Washington—even if you marry her. It's the law. The wording of this ordinance is such that it is a major crime to deflower a virgin—even if she is your wife. The law reads: "Every person who shall seduce and have sexual intercourse with any female of previously chaste character shall be punished by imprisonment in the state penitentiary for not more than five (5) years or in the county jail for not more than one (1) year or by a fine of $1000 or by both fine and imprisonment."

The *Duluth News Tribune* reported on July 17, 2009, the story of Christopher Bjerkness's arrest in Duluth, Minnesota, on charges of breaking into a gymnasium and slashing forty large rubber exercise balls. Bjerkness admitted in 2006, following a conviction of slashing seventy such exercise balls, that he has an unstoppable sexual urge to destroy the balls.

In Florida: "Whoever commits
any unnatural and lascivious act
with another person is guilty of
a misdemeanor. A mother's
breastfeeding of her baby does
not violate this section."

—*FLA. STAT. ANN § 800.02* (ENACTED 1993)

A Taiwanese woman went to the Taipei
Medical University hospital because she was
having trouble with her cell phone. Apparently,
during some bizarre sex game with her boyfriend,
the woman had gotten the cell phone lodged
in her bottom and couldn't get it out. Hospital
staffers theorized that the cell phone was inserted,
not for its hands-free feature, but for its vibrating
feature. After doctors successfully removed the
cell phone I wonder if they handed it to the
woman saying, "It's for you."

Minnesota's adultery law is great
if you're a lascivious male:
"Adultery occurs when a married
woman has sexual intercourse
with a man other than her husband,
whether the man is married or not. . . .
There is no prohibition against
sex between a married man and
an unmarried woman."

—MINN. STAT. § 609.36 (ENACTED 1963)

A twenty-four-year-old woman in Beloit, Wisconsin, was charged with battery for allegedly hitting her husband with a plant stand and sending him to the hospital for six stitches. According to the police statement, the newlyweds frequently fought about sex. The night of the attack the woman became enraged because her husband decided to call it quits after only four sexual encounters with her that day.

In Cottonwood, Alabama, it is against the law to have sex in a car with "flat wheels." The fine is increased if the act takes place in the backseat or while either offending party is driving the car at the time.

In order to assist in the county's safe-sex program, sixteen condom dispensers were installed at the San Francisco County Jail in San Bruno, California, according to a September 8, 2010, article in the *San Francisco Chronicle*—even though jailhouse sex is illegal.

In Colorado "It is a misdemeanor for an acupuncturist to engage in sexual contact, and a felony to engage in sexual intrusion or penetration, with a patient during the course of patient care."

—Colo. Rev. Stat. § 12-29.5-108 (enacted 1989)

sharks

Nearly fifty people noticed a shark in a cove in Somerset, Massachusetts, and several of them called 911 to report the sighting. When authorities arrived at the cove, however, they discovered that it wasn't a shark people had spotted: "It was Styrofoam shaped into a fin and wrapped with gray duct tape with weights holding it in place," said a police spokesman. According to a September 26, 2010, article in the *Herald News*, a prankster was preying on people's fears after several "actual shark sightings."

A British tourist didn't think anyone would believe his fish story so he brought the catch back to the hotel with him and placed it in the bathtub: a five-foot live shark.

While on a diving trip off the Florida Keys with his family, a sixteen-year-old Rockford, Illinois, youth became fascinated with a shark swimming nearby. So he did what any person who is underwater in the company of sharks would do—he pulled on the shark's tail. The shark, being a shark, did what any shark in the same situation would do—he chomped down on the boy's chest and wouldn't let go. The boy swam back to the diving vessel and was pulled aboard, shark still clinging on. The captain radioed the Coast Guard, which took the boy, and the shark, by boat and then on an ambulance ride to Fisherman's Hospital. A doctor had to split the three-foot nurse shark's spine in order to unlock its jaw. The teenager was released the same day; the shark didn't pull through.

sharks

After snorkeling off Caves Beach, north of Sydney, Australia, Luke Tresoglavic swam one thousand feet to shore, walked to his car, and drove to the local surf club to show everyone the shark he had brought with him. Lifeguards were stunned at the shark not because of its size but because it was attached to Tresoglavic's leg and wouldn't let go. They forced freshwater into the gills of the two-foot-long carpet shark until it eventually released his grip. Tresoglavic told Australian Broadcasting Corporation radio on February 11, 2004, that he was fine and didn't even require stitches, only a course of antibiotics, but that the shark didn't make it.

Tresoglavic reportedly buried the shark in his garden. I guess that's what happens when you become attached to an animal.

sheep | S

An unnamed Wanaka, New Zealand, man contacted police in the middle of the night to complain that there was a pregnant sheep sleeping in bed with him. When police arrived the sheep had already hoofed it and there were no traces of "wool or hoof marks in the bed." The complainant could not identify any distinguishing marks on the sheep, but police don't believe the man tried to pull the wool over their eyes. They told the man, who had admitted to being intoxicated the night before, that he was probably the victim of a prank—and to "give up the drink." The August 27, 2005, article from the New Zealand Press Association stated that police never inquired how the man knew the sheep was pregnant.

S

sheep

"If they can do that with faces, the implication is that they have to have reasonable intelligence; otherwise, what is the point of having a system for remembering faces and not remembering anything else?" asked behavioral scientist Keith Kendrick from the Babraham Institute in Cambridge, England. Sheep, who have traditionally been considered quite dim, actually have a very keen memory and can recognize as many as fifty other sheep for up to two years, according to an article in the November 7, 2001, issue of *National Geographic Today*. "It is a very sophisticated memory system," Kendrick said. "They are showing similar abilities in many ways to humans." Which isn't anything for which the sheep should be too proud.

According to a March 27, 2007, article in the *Raleigh News & Observer*, city officials notified David Watts of Apex, North Carolina, that the eighty sheep he had been keeping in his home as pets were going to be impounded. Neighbors had been tolerant of Watts's odd behavior, but when some of the sheep wandered out of his house and into a cemetery and ate fresh floral arrangements, they filed a complaint.

signs

Residents of Longmont, Colorado, voted in a resolution to abolish all "Dead End" signs and have them replaced with signs reading "No Outlet." The residents considered the "Dead End" signs too unpleasant. I wonder if they'll replace the "Slow Children" sign with "Speed-Sensitive Offspring."

In a Tokyo hotel:
"Is forbitten to steal hotel towels please.
If you are not person to do such thing is please
not to read notis."

In a Paris hotel elevator:
"Please leave your values at the front desk."

*In the lobby of a Moscow hotel across from a
Russian Orthodox monastery:*
"You are welcome to visit the cemetery where
famous Russian and Soviet composers, artists, and
writers are buried daily except Thursday."

* * *

On the menu of a Swiss restaurant:
"Our wines leave you nothing to hope for."

* * *

In a Hong Kong supermarket:
"For your convenience, we recommend courteous, efficient self-service."

* * *

On the door of a Moscow hotel room:
"If this is your first visit to the USSR, you are welcome to it."

* * *

Two signs from a Majorcan shop entrance:
"English well talking" and
"Here speeching American."

* * *

A sign posted in Germany's Black Forest:
It is strictly forbidden on our black forest camping site that people of different sex, for instance, men and women, live together in one tent unless they are married with each other for that purpose.

snakes

S

Michael Dean Messer of Waynesville, North Carolina, was taking one of his pets out for a stroll because he was worried after his "dog got him upset." In an article in the *Asheville Citizen-Times*, August 17, 2001, the pet Messer had taken outside "for some exercise" was a four-foot-long timber rattlesnake. Messer reported that he was "worried about him [not] eating" so he charmed the snake into eating a hen's egg. Going against the rule that says you shouldn't bite the hand that feeds you, the snake bit him.

"MAN ACCUSED OF BITING GIRLFRIEND'S SNAKE"

—ASSOCIATED PRESS HEADLINE, AUGUST 24, 2007

A baby rattlesnake bit Travis Williams, a student at Salt Lake City High School, after Williams was warned not to pick it up. According to a May 8, 2005, Associated Press article, Williams admitted he was more rattled than the snake: "I picked it up even though she told me not to. . . . I'm not too bright that way."

Continental Airlines settled with the parents of five-year-old Alexandra Taylor for an undisclosed sum because the pet of another passenger had terrified the little girl during a flight in 1994, causing her to have recurring nightmares. Continental had allowed a female passenger to bring aboard a six-foot-long python that served as a "support snake" to help the woman overcome her fear of flying.

"SNAKE FOUND IN HAWAII-BOUND PASSENGER'S PANTS"

—ASSOCIATED PRESS HEADLINE, FEBRUARY 6, 2003

Charles Page was driving down Golden Gate Parkway in Naples, Florida, when he noticed a man in another car struggling with what looked like a rope around his neck. But what thirty-year-old Courtland Page Johnson was actually fighting with was his four-foot boa constrictor, which was coiled around his neck and had bitten his face. Johnson jumped out of his PT Cruiser after he had banged into several roadside barricades, untangled himself from the snake, and then quickly slithered away. Police located Johnson at his house after the March 28, 2006, accident. He was arrested and charged with leaving the scene of a crash and taken to the Naples Jail Center.

S

snakes

Two men, Joe Buddy Caine of Edwardsville, Alabama, and his friend Junior Bright had been drinking when they came across a four-foot rattlesnake. So they decided the fun thing to do would be to pick the snake up and toss it back and forth to each other. Surprisingly, the snake didn't see the fun and bit Bright on the hand. Then, when Caine tried to kill it, the snake bit Caine on the hand. The two men called 911, and when paramedics arrived both were in a semiconscious state (although it seems to me that they were in a semiconscious state to begin with). Caine went into cardiac arrest on the ambulance ride to the hospital and died about an hour after being bitten. We could learn a valuable lesson from these two men: Don't drink and toss snakes!

A small copperhead snake slithered up to the unsuspecting Sam Pettengill in Poolesville, Maryland, and bit him several times on the hand. The usual impulse for most people would be to kill the snake and then go to the hospital for treatment. But Pettengill was in a Buddhist temple and, as he was a practicing Buddhist, he picked up the snake and circled a prayer room three times to bless it before releasing it, unharmed, back into the wild. According to a June 3, 2009, article in the *Washington Post*, Pettengill then sought medical attention in the form of four antivenin cycles.

A fter emerging from a three-day coma, Matt Wilkinson admitted during a September 19, 2007, interview with KGW-TV of Portland, Oregon, that he had stuck his pet Eastern diamondback rattlesnake into his mouth while drinking with some buddies. "Me, being me, I put his head in my mouth," Wilkinson admitted. He claimed that the incident was "kind of" his "own stupid fault." A doctor determined that Wilkinson was lucky to have made it to the hospital on time as the venomous bites had nearly caused his airway to completely swell shut.

Operators at 911 centers have received
complaints about clogged toilets before,
but the call the Mesa, Arizona, 911 dispatchers
received from Jona Giammalva rattled even them.
Giammalva was angry at her children because she
thought they had flushed one of their toys down
the toilet. Try as she might, Giammalva couldn't
get the toilet to flush properly. She had tried drain
clearer, a wire coat hanger, and a plunger. She
had heard the term "snaking" out a pipe to get it
clean—but this isn't what she had counted on.

Finally, after several tries, Giammalva saw
something slowing emerging from the toilet. Was
it a piece of Lego? A small truck, perhaps? She
leaned in closer to get a better look and was soon
face-to-face with a huge boa constrictor. "I was
out of there in a split second," Giammalva said.
"I wasn't about to waste any time." She quickly
called 911 and was referred to a wildlife expert,
who soon had the toilet bowl boa out of the
bathroom and out of Giammalva's house. Both
the snake and Giammalva let out a sigh of relief.
How cruel to have a snake in your toilet right
after you've gotten the crap scared out of you.

squirrels

City officials in Santa Monica, California, announced a really squirrelly plan in 2005 that made it unnecessary for male squirrels to hide their nuts anymore. The city administered birth-control shots to the city's squirrels using GonaCon, a serum that halts ovulation in female squirrels and testicular development in males. The makers of the drug say the shot, which cost about two to ten dollars per dose, does not have any dangerous side effects—but apparently no one asked the squirrels about that. Researchers say the shot takes about three months to take effect. I wonder if any moral conservatives protested the inoculations on the grounds that it would promote promiscuity among the sterile squirrel community.

911 REPORT:
Male complainant called to inform that there is a squirrel on his front porch.

S

squirrels

It was a hostage situation. Seattle, Washington, police officer Steve Oskierko was the first on the scene—summoned by an emergency 911 phone call. He peered in through the glass doors of the John L. Scott real-estate office and spotted the hostages. There were more than fifty office workers trembling in fear as the enraged hostage taker paced menacingly in front of them. The hostages were in the back of the building—some holding boxes, others holding their coats, all of them trying to keep from being attacked by the savage red-headed wild-eyed . . . squirrel.

This wasn't your typical furry, nut-loving little creature—this crazed critter had already attacked one woman and was harassing others. The hostages breathed a sigh of relief when they saw Officer Oskierko outside their office. "They kept saying, 'Get it out of here, get it out of here,'" Oskierko said. Oskierko slowly entered the premises. When the squirrel's back was turned

Oskierko made a lunge at him—and the hostages heard a loud tear: Oskierko's pants had split during the assault. He radioed for reinforcements (both for himself and his pants).

squirrels

Other officers arrived and soon they had the cagey culprit captive. The police turned the furry felon over to a veterinarian who planned to examine the squirrel for rabies. But iron bars do not a prison make, and for this little woodland creature a plastic cage didn't make a very good one, either. He nibbled and gnawed his way through the cage, attacked the vet and others, and escaped. The squirrel is still on the lam.

stupidity

The *Merced (CA) Sun-Star* reported on December 10, 2002, that police were called to investigate an incident involving an unnamed man was who taken to a Modesto, California, hospital after his head was split open by a brick. Eyewitnesses quickly made it clear to police investigators that the victim was the one who was actually as thick as a brick. Apparently the man had tossed the brick into the air at 2:30 a.m. to see how high he could throw it and, as it was dark, lost sight of it until it clomped down on his head. Obviously the guy was a real blockhead.

According to a May 21, 2003, news report on Philadelphia, Pennsylvania's NBCPhiladelphia.com, a thirty-eight-year-old man from Pine Creek Valley, Delaware, suffered burns to his head and arms when he attempted to dispose of gunpowder by tossing it onto the burning logs in his fireplace.

In 2001, Phyllis A. Engleson filed a federal lawsuit against the city of Little Falls, Minnesota, for damages she suffered when she tripped over an orange traffic cone during the city's 1998 Arts and Craft Fair. Engleson claimed she was not at fault and that the city should have provided a warning that there were orange traffic cones ahead. The lawsuit was ultimately dismissed in 2004 by Judge Donovan Frank, who stated that the purpose of the bright orange traffic cone is to warn people of imminent risk. The dismissal stated, "She did not see any of the traffic cones before her fall. They were twenty-eight inches tall, had two reflector collars, and were placed at sixty-foot intervals so as six or seven lined each side of the street in a given block." The dismissal also stated that it isn't the city's responsibility "to provide visitors warning upon warning, ad infinitum."

Kyle Dubois, a New Hampshire teenager, was in his electrical trades class when he and fellow students decided to attach clamps to his nipples and plug them into an active electrical cord. According to an August 31, 2010, Associated Press article, Dubois suffered permanent brain damage as a result of his actions. Five months later, Dubois's parents sued both the school district and the shop teacher.

suicide | S

Nathan Ryan of Chandler, Arizona, had his suicide all worked out. He had the tip of a twenty-four-inch sword tied to his steering wheel and pointing at his chest. He drove head-on into a wall. What he didn't realize was that his car would crash through the wall and that a swimming pool was waiting for him on the other side.

According to a June 19, 2009, article in the *Tucson East Valley Tribune*, when the car hit the wall the airbag deployed, bending the sword away from his heart, and Ryan was able to swim to the surface.

"I think I'd just commit suicide."

—SENATOR JOHN MCCAIN (R-AZ), ON OCTOBER 18, 2006, ANTICIPATING HIS POSSIBLE REACTION TO THE DEMOCRATS TAKING BACK THE SENATE IN THE NOVEMBER 2006 ELECTION. (THEY DID—HE DIDN'T.)

Crown Point, Indiana, police reopened the case of a man who died from thirty-two hammer blows to his head. Police had initially ruled the cause of death as a suicide. The county coroner's opinion, however, was that a person could not remain conscious long enough to hit himself in the head thirty-two times.

"I was expecting the worst," said police communications unit director Frieda Lehner about a suicide call she received through the Albuquerque police headquarters. She engaged the caller in a conversation and tried to talk the man out of any rash moves. They discussed his divorce and custody battle, his tour in Vietnam, and how he finally wound up living with his mother because he was unable to get a job, even though he looked.

Lehner recalled that the man grew more and more agitated about how rotten his life had become. Suddenly, and to her horror, a gunshot was heard over the phone line. Lehner heard the phone drop—and then there was silence. Soon she could hear the rustling of the phone being picked back up.

"He came back on the line and he was extremely upset. He was using some very good adjectives. I asked, 'Are you hurt?' He said, 'I just shot my mother's favorite pillow. She's going to kill me.'

"That one was very stressful, but it turned out real good." Sounds like to me if the guy really wanted to kill himself he should have shot his mother's favorite pillow first and just waited.

According to a September 27, 2003, Associated Press article, a sixty-six-year-old woman from Menlo Park, California, Mrs. Jessie Brockman, was thwarted in her attempt to commit suicide—she had a heart attack and died of natural causes before she could pull the trigger.

According to Indiana police, Mark Weinberger, a plastic surgeon from Merrillville, ripped off a number of his patients by recommending they have expensive and unnecessary plastic surgery, or misdiagnosed them, botched their surgeries, or hastily performed the wrong procedures. When hundreds of patients and insurance companies started filing lawsuits against him he packed up some survival gear and ran, leaving behind his wife and more than $5 million in debt. Five years later, Weinberger was discovered in Italy hiding in a tent at six thousand feet on Mont Blanc. According to a December 17, 2009, Huffington Post article, after his arrest, Weinberger took out a box cutter and slit his own throat, but missed all critical arteries and survived.

"I want to sue them. They have caused me more misery than I felt before," said forty-five-year-old Victor Dodoi from Botosani in northern Moldavia, Romania. Dodoi wanted to sue the manufacturer of a rope he had used in a botched suicide attempt, according to a February 27, 2003, article in the Romanian tabloid newspaper *Libertatea*. Dodoi had tied the rope to a light fixture in his living room, but the rope broke under his weight and brought the light and part of the ceiling crashing down on top of him.

Mechanic Gerald Marotta of El Sereno, California, was depressed after the state enacted a law in January 1992 requiring all motorcyclists to wear helmets. Marotta, whose wife said always rode his motorcycle helmetless as a means of relaxing and dealing with problems, shot himself to death several days after the law went into effect. A portion of his suicide note read "Now I can't even ride."

synchronicity

The April 13, 2005, edition of London's *Telegraph* told of the bizarre fatal automobile accident involving Alison Taylor and her Peugeot. The Peugeot wouldn't start, so Taylor pulled out a hammer to tap on the starter as it obviously had a dead spot and wouldn't turn over. She had done this before, but this time she left the keys in the ignition. When the starter engaged, the car sprang to life and, as she had also left the car in gear, it began rolling over her. As a reflex she instinctively grabbed something—unfortunately, it was the throttle cable. The car accelerated, dragging Taylor with it, and eventually went over an embankment. The coroner in North Tyneside, England, declared the cause of Taylor's death an accident.

Tim Brender "knew he needed to start getting things organized," said his wife, Lani, of their upcoming move. So the Madison, Wisconsin, man went down into the basement of his rented townhouse to start packing. He moved a table, which knocked over a can of spray paint that fell on a hammer lying on the floor. The claw of the hammer punctured the spray paint can, which started spraying like an out-of-control garden hose. The can spun around and squirted paint on the pilot light of the hot water heater. The flame roared up and set fire to a cushion and quickly spread to a container of gunpowder. From there things just got worse, and eventually the fire consumed everything in the house. Lani was quoted in the April 9, 2005, edition of the *Madison Capital Times* as saying, "You couldn't set up this scenario to happen." To which I would reply, "Why would you?"

synchronicity

tasers

Police were called to the residence of Brian Mattert in Cheyenne, Wyoming, to investigate a complaint of domestic violence. When they arrived, the thirty-four-year-old man quickly poured white latex paint all over himself and yelled at the arresting officers, "You see all this water-based paint? You shoot me with that [Taser] and you'll kill me." The officers tried to explain to Mattert that paint would have no effect on the Taser one way or the other, but he continued to be belligerent.

They eventually shocked him. Mattert, of course, didn't die and, according to a September 25, 2010, Associated Press article, was arrested and charged with domestic violence, assault and battery, resisting arrest, and aggravated assault on a police officer.

"POLICE TASER MAN WITH CHICKEN IN CAR"

—Associated Press headline, September 18, 2007

Twenty-two-year-old Charles Littleton angrily refused to remove his Los Angeles Dodgers baseball cap during a Saginaw, Michigan, City Council meeting. According to a report from Flint, Michigan, television station WJRT, Littleton said, "It means more than just a hat. It's like my crown. It's like asking a king to remove his crown." Littleton became defiant after he was asked to either remove his hat or leave and was eventually subdued by police with a stun gun.

The shock heard around the world: On September 17, 2007, U.S. senator John Kerry addressed a Constitution Day forum at the University of Florida in Gainesville, and was questioned by twenty-one-year-old Andrew Meyer. Meyer's questioning became more pointed, and two University of Florida police officers attempted to take him away. It was then that he uttered the immortal line: "Don't tase me, bro!"

They "tased" him anyway.

tasers

T

Forty-two-year-old Robert McClain of Royal Oak, Michigan, literally went medieval on police officers when they arrived at his home after he had fled the scene of an automobile accident. The police were met at the door by McClain, who held them at bay by brandishing a four-foot sword. He then ran to the basement as he was pursued. McClain put on a chain mail vest and leather gauntlets and started swinging a giant wooden mallet. He taunted the officers by saying, "I have a thousand years of power." The officers, however, had a Taser with a thousand volts of power that knocked McClain on his medieval butt. According to the August 5, 2005, police records posted on TheSmokingGun.com, McClain was arrested and charged with felony assault and leaving the scene of an accident. No word on whether he was charged with misdemeanor geek.

tattoos

"It's a brilliant icebreaker," said Ian Roberson of Treharris, Glamorgan, in Wales. "Now when I meet women I just ask the girls if they want to see my plums and roll up my sleeve." What he reveals when he rolls up his sleeve is a tattoo. But it's not an eagle or the word "Mom" or a heart with an arrow through it—it's a can of tomatoes.

When Ian's wife, Susan, walked out after ten years of marriage, she not only left him brokenhearted but also with only a can of Princes plum tomatoes in the kitchen. The story of the tin of tomatoes brought a lot of canned laughter to Ian's friends at the pub, so he decided to stop stewing and have some fun. "Now every time I look at the tattoo it reminds me of the day my wife walked out," Ian said.

But the can of tomatoes on his arm wasn't put there just to symbolize the tomato that walked out of his life—Ian also had it done on the condition that his pub friends help him raise £500 for a villager suffering from a rare form of cancer. I'm sure other people have noticed that the name "Princes" doesn't just refer to the name on the tomato can.

Dominique Fisher, a "tattooist," and her new boyfriend, Wayne Robinson, had been on a four-day drinking binge. While he was sleeping it off she carved out a new life for him—with a box cutter. Robinson was surprised and angry when he awoke to find that Fisher had carved her name and other marks on his body. According to a January 29, 2009, article in the *Lancashire Telegraph*, Fisher exclaimed to Robinson, "I thought you'd like it." Apparently he didn't as he took her to Britain's Burnley Crown Court where she received probation.

The *Denver Post* ran a story on September 2, 2003, about a twenty-year-old man who was killed during afternoon rush hour when he leaped from a car going about 40 mph. According to the victim's friends, the man had been planning on jumping for a while but not to kill himself—he thought enduring the pain would give him the courage to get a tattoo. Unfortunately, the only ink the man got was a small blurb in the newspaper— and then again in the obituary column.

"I guess my girl wasn't meant to have 3-D breasts," remarked Edmonton, Alberta, tattoo artist Lane Jensen. Jensen had tattooed a buxom cowgirl on his left calf and wanted to augment her with silicon "implants." According to a February 18, 2008, article in the *Edmonton Sun*, within two weeks the fluid leaked and had to be drained.

Eduardo Arrocha performed for fifteen years as "Eak the Geek," the "Pain-Proof Man" at New York's Coney Island Sideshow, where he ate lightbulbs, walked on glass, snapped mousetraps on his tongue, and lay on nails. But as told in the September 4, 2007, edition of the *Los Angeles Times*, Arrocha traded in his glamorous showbiz life for a seat in Thomas M. Cooley Law School in Lansing, Michigan. Arrocha, at the time a second-year student who went from "one freak show to another," as he put it, admitted that "it's the most bizarre thing I've ever done in my life." He said he realized that job interviews would be difficult as he had to hide his chest-to-toe tattoos. However, recruiters wouldn't be able to miss the stars and planets that were tattooed over his entire face.

T **F**ederal officers in Billings, Montana, spotted fugitive Sterling Wolfname on the street, and when they approached him he tried to give them an alias. The twenty-six-year-old didn't fool the officers, however, because, according to an August 14, 2008, Associated Press article, "Wolfname" was tattooed on the side of his head.

When Dan O'Connor left a tattoo parlor in Carlstadt, New Jersey, he had a proud look on his face and a new tattoo on his arm. He loved Notre Dame and had decided to express his passion by spending $125 to have a tattoo of the "Fighting Irish" leprechaun permanently etched into his skin. But when he looked down to admire the tattoo artist's handiwork, he noticed something was wrong. Instead of reading "Fighting Irish," the tattoo read "Fighing Irish"— the "t" had been left out. O'Connor was "fighing" mad and filed suit against the tattoo parlor in 1996 saying, "I can't just live with this. You're not talking about a dented car where you can get another one. You're talking about flesh."

teachers

Colleagues said they tolerated the bizarre behavior of a first-grade teacher in Pine Grove Elementary School in Brooksville, Florida, for months but didn't have sufficient grounds to fire her until she finally cracked—by dropping her pants and mooning everyone at a staff meeting. According to a February 1, 2005, article in the *St. Petersburg Times*, Susan Bartlett was considered "out of control," was accused of smoking pot, "burped loudly" to disrupt staff meetings, and "yell[ed] at the kids all the time," using words like "butt" and "stupid." After Bartlett literally showed her ass, she was ordered to take a drug test, which she refused, claiming there was a "lack of just cause." School board members therefore demanded her resignation. I'm not sure about you, but she sounds like a pretty fun teacher to me.

T

In 1995, Connecticut judge Socrates Mihalakos ruled that Nancy Sekor, a middle school teacher who was fired from her job in 1993 for incompetence, had to be reinstated. His reasoning? Sekor had been judged incompetent in only two of the three subjects she taught.

According to a September 12, 2007, article in the *Mobile Register*, an unnamed Alabama teacher who had been fired from his position but was awaiting trial on a charge of raping a student, had continued to receive his regular paycheck for the previous two years and would continue receiving it until the trial was over. What makes the matter more outrageous is that he had also been awarded two mandatory pay raises, keeping with a 2004 state law on teacher's rights.

"STUDENT RUNS OVER DRIVER'S ED TEACHER"

—Associated Press headline, February 12, 2005

teachers

An elementary school teacher from Palm Harbor, Florida, was arrested on suspicion of driving under the influence and was dismissed from her job. The woman successfully beat the conviction and was therefore reinstated by the school board. The woman argued, apparently convincingly, that the reason she appeared disoriented during the stop wasn't because she was drunk but because a silicone breast implant had ruptured and poisoned her nervous system. Now if Pamela Anderson is ever pulled over she'll know she has a full set of excuses.

"STUDENT MAY BE SUSPENDED FOR STRANGLING HIS TEACHER"

—STAR (MALAYSIA) HEADLINE, JULY 28, 2007

T

A science experiment at Winona High School in Texas turned out to be a real blast. A seventeen-year-old student, with the approval of his physics teacher, brought in a homemade cannon designed to use gunpowder that "shoots a little projectile in the air," said school superintendent Rodney Fausett. But when the metal tube was being loaded with the gunpowder it exploded—sending the "small little tube . . . through the wall of the building—a metal wall—so it had a pretty good oomph to it," said an investigator from the U.S. Bureau of Alcohol, Tobacco, Firearms, and Explosives. According to a May 19, 2006, article in the *Dallas Morning News*, parents had expressed concern over the demonstration but school officials blew them off.

telephones

Cincinnati-based Kroger Company pulled specially designed cereal boxes featuring Bengals star Chad Ochocinco because of a typo in the phone number for Feed the Children. The number was supposed to be 1-888-HELP-FTC, which connects to Feed the Children, the charity the cereal was supporting, but customers who attempted to call the number listed on the box, 1-800-HELP-FTC, were instead connected with a phone sex line, reported an October 3, 2010, Associated Press article. The mistake quickly made the cereal go from corn flakes to porn flakes.

T

A call came into the 911 center and paramedics were immediately on their way to an "abdominal evisceration." The paramedics suited up in high-risk gloves, face shields, and other emergency gear in order to keep them safe. When they arrived at the residence, they found a thirteen-year-old boy lying on the bed motionless. They quickly examined the boy looking for a wound but couldn't find anything wrong. When they asked the boy why he had called 911, he told them because he had "stuff" coming out of his naval. Further investigation revealed the "stuff" to be belly-button lint.

On November 20, 1999, Reuters covered the announcement by Steven Slootsky, a lawyer for a former Fort Lauderdale, Florida, phone-sex worker, that he had won a workers' compensation settlement for his client. Slottsky's client declined to be identified because she suffered from carpal tunnel syndrome, on both hands, caused by masturbating on the job as many as seven times a day.

Talk about getting your lines crossed! A Japanese man, Yoshinori Sato, agreed to a blind date with Hiromi Mikado, a woman who had called him at a telephone dating club, and they arranged to meet in front of a cream puff store (not making this up, folks). They checked into a "Saitama love hotel," and Mikado asked if Sato was up for a little S&M. He agreed. Mikado blindfolded the man and ordered him to lie facedown on the bed. She then reached under the bed and pulled out a nylon cord and strangled him to death. When she was arrested she simply explained, "I don't know why he died" and later said, "I just wanted to kill somebody." In a little cruel irony, the incident was reported on Valentine's Day 2004 in the *Mainichi Daily News*.

T

tests

The following are actual answers to questions on science exams.

Q: Name the four seasons.

A: Salt, pepper, mustard, and vinegar.

Q: Explain one of the processes by which water can be made safe to drink.

A: Flirtation makes water safe to drink because it removes large pollutants like grit, sand, dead sheep, and canoeists.

Q: How is dew formed?

A: The sun shines down on the leaves and makes them perspire.

Q: How can you delay milk turning sour?

A: Keep it in the cow.

Q: What causes the tides in the oceans?

A: The tides are a fight between the earth and the moon. All water tends to flow toward the moon, because there is no water on the moon, and nature hates vacuum. I forget where the sun joins in this fight.

Q: What are steroids?

A: Things for keeping carpets still on the stairs.

Q: What happens to your body as you age?

A: When you get old, so do your bowels and you get inter-continental.

T trains

A malfunction during the switch-over from track power to the overhead power lines prompted a conductor on a Grand Central commuter train in New York to stop the train and climb up top with a fire extinguisher to investigate. According to a February 2008 article in the *White Plains Journal News*, it was fortunate that he took the fire extinguisher because a man, thirty-six-year-old Ricardo Chavez, had burst into flames from the eleven to fourteen thousand volts surging through the overhead lines. The conductor put out the torched train hopper and Chavez was hospitalized in fair condition—no word, however, on why he was on top of the train to begin with.

According to a Tallahassee, Florida, city ordinance, no train "is permitted to run through the city at a speed faster than an ordinary citizen can walk."

A twenty-five-year-old woman in Mount Prospect, Illinois, lost the toes on her right foot when she decided to crawl under a slow-moving train as a shortcut to the correct platform.

P olice in Brisbane, Australia, arrested a woman for dangerous driving after she ended up on a set of railroad tracks behind a train. The woman, who was driving at night with her daughter, told police she had taken a wrong turn, ended up on the tracks, and began tailgating the train "honking her car horn at the train as she followed it for 300 meters before being stuck on the tracks."

T

trains

According to an article in the April 22, 2003, edition of the Russian newspaper *Pravda*, a group of Russian train conductors came up with a unique contest as a way of whiling away the hours during their three-thousand-mile journey from Novosibirsk in Siberia to Vladivostok. Did they arm wrestle? No. Did they see who could belch the loudest? No. Did they see who had the strongest forehead by smashing it repeatedly against a train window? Yes. The contest was a tie as they were forced to stop midway through their journey to seek medical attention. I wonder if they were competing over the title of "head conductor."

According to a New York State law, "Each train must be preceded by a courier afoot or on a horse," in order to announce its approach to citizens.

Police in Los Angeles speculated that a twenty-one-year-old man deliberately parked his car, with his girlfriend inside, on a set of train tracks as a train was approaching. The man jumped out of the car moments before impact. Even though the train obliterated the car, the woman survived. According to a May 22, 2007, article in the *Los Angeles Times*, however, the car literally exploded into hundreds of sharp pieces of flying shrapnel—which struck and killed the man as he was running from the scene.

A young woman in Hamlin, West Virginia, needed to make a call on her cell phone and decided to follow safe-driving guidelines by pulling off the road. Unfortunately, the area of the road in which she chose to pull off, according to a January 8, 2003, *Lincoln Journal* article, was already occupied by two sets of train tracks. Before her call was connected, an oncoming train connected with her car and flung it onto the other set of tracks. The woman's train of thought was again put off track when another train, traveling in the other direction, smashed into her car from that side. Surprisingly the woman survived both train collisions.

U

underwear

According to a June 13, 2009, article in the *St. Petersburg Times*, the city council of Brooksville, Florida, adopted, by a four-to-one vote, a policy that requires that not only must all municipal employees wear underwear while on the job but that said underwear must not be visible.

According to an August 23, 2002, Associated Press article, a nineteen-year-old man was scheduled for trial for allegedly shooting another man at a concert in retaliation for the victim having given him a wedgie.

A pproximately twenty female students from Salinas High School in California held a protest at school upon hearing that the school's dress code banned thong underwear. "We wear thongs!" chanted the protesters. The demonstration finally broke up with the principal explaining that the school's dress code does not, and never has, banned thong underwear.

A n invention from Japan is sure to be a hit with more modest Japanese women. Keiko Yoshida, a Tokyo fabrics worker, announced that she had invented women's underwear that automatically shreds itself in extremely hot water. Yoshida created the underwear because of government regulations that require all garbage to be packaged in transparent bags. She believes a lot of Japanese women would rather have their old underwear dissolved than be seen by passersby.

Now that these underwear are on the market, I wonder if warm water contests will take the place of wet T-shirt contests.

U

underwear

Police officers pulled over an eighteen-year-old motorist who was driving erratically. The man bolted from his car and police pursued him on foot, caught him, and placed him in the back of their patrol car to take him downtown for a Breathalyzer test. Once he was alone in the backseat the young man knew he had to do something, so he ripped the crotch out of his underwear and stuffed it into his mouth, believing that the cotton would absorb all the alcohol. It didn't. He failed the test and was arrested. Ultimately he was acquitted of drunken driving charges, but his testimony caused so much laughter in the courtroom that many members of the court had to be escorted out in tears. I'm glad the accused man didn't offer anything on which to wipe their eyes.

undignified

According to an August 2, 2002, article in the *Sacramento Bee*, a forty-seven-year-old man in Aptos, California, died after he lost his balance while removing his pants, hopped over to a window on the second story of his home, and accidentally fell out.

Army veteran Erik Beelman was shot to death by marine veteran Christopher Marlowe in New Orleans, reported the *Times-Picayune* on June 28, 2006, following an argument over which branch of the military is tougher.

Emmanuel Nieves was charged with aggravated assault by police in Mansfield Township and Hackettstown, New Jersey, according to November 15, 2002, article in the *Easton Express-Times*, after slashing the face of his friend Erik Saporito following an argument they had over which one had the hairiest butt.

U

Kenneth Ware allegedly stabbed his brother to death in Brooklyn, New York, according to a July 12, 2003, *New York Post* article, because he wouldn't return his New York Yankees cap.

During a fight at a community center in Calgary, Alberta, a man in his twenties was killed, according to a May 18, 2009, article from the Canadian Broadcasting Corporation, following a dominoes tournament.

Three coworkers of a sixty-year-old man who was retiring from a transportation company in Ritto, Japan, playfully tossed him into the air in celebration. According to a December 16, 2008, article in the *Mainichi Daily News*, while the man was in midair there was a miscommunication between the three as to who was going to catch him. The celebrant struck the ground and was killed instantly.

A twenty-one-year-old man fishing off Jones Beach on New York's Long Island apparently yanked his line back too quickly, launching his three-ounce lead sinker out of the water with great force. According to July 29, 2008, article in *Newsday*, he was killed when the sinker sunk into his skull and penetrated his brain.

A s reported in the August 9, 2008, edition of the *Wilmington Star News*, an unexpected gust of wind in Leland, North Carolina, pulled a canopy umbrella out of its holder and propelled it through the air. The tip lodged into the skull of a thirty-two-year-old man lounging beside a pool.

"The male claimed he was not being chased," the Seattle police report notes, "but rather he thought he was a ninja and would be able to successfully leap over the four-to-five-foot fence." According to a November 17, 2009, article in the *Seattle Post-Intelligencer*, the man failed in his attempt to jump the fence, impaled himself on a top spike, and had to be rescued by Seattle Fire Department.

U

undignified

U unexplainable

Police were called to New Bentham Court, Ecclesbourne Road, in Islington in North London following up on a report of a young man on fire. When police and fire crews arrived, they discovered the youth in a front garden, engulfed in flames, and quickly put the fire out. The seventeen-year-old boy was rushed to a hospital suffering from severe burns. The BBC reported on September 29, 2007, that detectives investigating the case say they do not know if the boy had set himself on fire or if an attack is suspected.

According to a June 3, 2001, article in the *St. Louis Post-Dispatch*, weeks after a man collapsed and died during a meeting of a Milwaukee, Wisconsin, chapter of Alcoholics Anonymous his identity was still a mystery as people attending meetings usually do so anonymously.

On February 17, 2003, Leonia, New Jersey, resident Selimy Mensah was hospitalized with second- and third-degree burns to her face and hands after a fire broke out in her apartment. According to police, the fire started when Mensah tried to open a can of aerosol spray paint with an electric can opener.

U

unexplainable

U urine

Larry Ray Pratt was the first person in Johnson County, Kansas, charged under a new food-supply protection law (The Bioterrorism Act of 2002) and convicted of criminal trespass and criminal damage to property, both misdemeanors. Pratt was arrested after employees of a Dillons Store identified his photograph in a lineup and he was sentenced to ten days in jail and a year on probation. An article in the July 11, 2003, *Topeka Capital-Journal* reported that Pratt's act of bioterrorism consisted of him urinating on packages of chicken in a supermarket cooler. Pratt now belongs to a long line of terrorists who are considered yellow-bellied chickens.

Arrested in West Haven, Connecticut, for spitting on a police officer and urinating in his patrol car: **Ms. Lonna Leak.**

—*New Haven Register*, September 20, 2000

According to a June 16, 2003, article in the *Houston Chronicle*, a twenty-three-year-old man needed to answer the call of nature so he opened the passenger door of a pickup truck to urinate. Unfortunately, the truck was speeding down Houston's Southwest Freeway at the time and the man fell out, was run over, and died.

During his unsuccessful race for county commissioner in Tallahassee, Florida, local weatherman Mike Rucker apologized for urinating in a voter's yard in October 2002. Rucker claimed the incident was caused by a prostate problem—not that he was angry because the person refused to put Rucker's campaign sign in their yard. Now, if Rucker had been a yellow-dog Democrat this activity might have made more sense.

The *Mainichi Daily News* reported on May 18, 2007, that a neighbor's house in Osaka, Japan, was blocking the view Hiroshi Nishizaki so treasured. In a plot to get the neighbor to move, Nishizaki poured urine on the offending house on 169 occasions before he was caught. He is accused of causing damage to the house in the amount of $5,500.

V | values

Sheila Chapman and Ray Reed of Tampa, Florida, celebrated "Prince" Clayburn Reed's birthday by inviting sixty guests (including a professional party planner) to a shindig that included pony rides, a magician, and a piñata, all nestled in a rented room at their local country club. According to a February 24, 2008, article in the *St. Petersburg Times*, Chapman told a reporter: "These are the memories I want him to have. I want him to know how important and special I think he is."

"Prince" was celebrating his one-year birthday.

"**M**y campaign is not based on a foundation of lies," said twenty-one-year-old Antwon Womack, a candidate for the Board of Education in Birmingham, Alabama. "My values are not lies. It's just the information I provided to the people is false." His campaign Web site included many falsehoods, including his age (he claimed to be twenty-three); that he had graduated from Alabama A&M with the title of "Dr." (he dropped out of high school as a freshman); and that he had chaired three previous political campaigns (he hadn't). Even his phone number and address were wrong—because he didn't live in the district where he was running.

Womack promised to drop out of the race but later reneged, claiming that two local politicians supported his candidacy—which they didn't and demanded he stop referring to them. According to an August 19, 2002, article in the *Birmingham News*, Womack came in third with just 117 votes.

V

values

It was named the "rat-out rule" and it does just that, according to school board chairman Sam Pennington of Friendship, Maine. "I'll admit that we're ordering students to tattle on their friends," says Pennington. The rule requires students to "promptly report any violation of the rules . . . [at] school or school-sponsored events. Students or staff must not withhold information or fail to report rumors or threats to school officials."

Students who do not follow the letter of the law "will be disciplined, up to and including suspension." According to the *Portland News-Herald*, Pennington is now working on the next item of business: compiling a list of the "core values" the district must teach all students. "I'm sure trust is one of the values we will adopt," he said.

Forty-two-year-old Leslie Collard was arrested in Providence, Rhode Island, after offering an undercover officer a two-for-one deal: Collard promised sexual favors for pay for both herself and her nineteen-year-old daughter. According to a May 3, 2002, article in the *Providence Journal*, when the undercover officer asked if the tandem offer meant mother and daughter would service him simultaneously, she exclaimed, "No. I have morals, because she is my daughter. My daughter will do you first."

Little seven-year-old Brandy McKenith of Stanton Heights, Pennsylvania, heard a boy at school quietly exclaim, "I swear to God." McKenith knew that swearing to God wasn't a good thing so she told him, "You're going to go to hell for swearing to God." Hell unleashed itself, all right—for McKenith, who was suspended from Sunnyside Elementary for a day because of "profanity" rules. Her father, police detective Wayne McKenith said, "Kids are bringing guns and knives to school. They've got dope. And we're worried about 'hell'?"

S elf-described fiscal conservative Republican Larry Schwarz, a Colorado state legislator from 1995 to 1997 and then a parole board member, changed jobs in 2004 to become a warehouse manager and bookkeeper for his stepdaughter's pornography business. His stepdaughter, a retired porn actress who went by the stage name Jewel De'Nyle, formed Platinum X Pictures in Canoga Park, California, where she also employs her mother. As reported in an August 7, 2004, article in the *Rocky Mountain News*, Schwarz continues to believe in his "Republican ideals of self-reliance, lower taxes, and individual freedom."

According to court documents, local police raided Schwarz's home on December 4, 2001, looking for child pornography and removed cartoon books depicting children having sex and other items, including tapes of De'Nyle. Police also investigated claims that Schwarz had sexually molested family members years earlier. No charges were filed, but Governor Bill Owens fired him from the parole board.

vomit

V

Both teams were in their stance. The ball was ready to be snapped. The quarterback was calling out the signals. Denver Bronco defensive tackle Darren Drozdov was in his position opposite the offensive center. During those tense few milliseconds before the ball went into play during this August 1993 game, Drozdov made a messy defensive foul—he vomited on the ball. After the game Drozdov told reporters, "I get sick a lot. I was a quarterback in high school, and I'd start throwing up on my center's back. I don't have a lot of control out there." Well, at least his heart is in the right place.

W waitresses

Professor Michael Lynn, who teaches marketing and tourism at Cornell University in Ithaca, New York, surveyed 374 waitresses and came to some startling conclusions. According to a May 7, 2010, article in the *Cornell Daily Sun*, Lynn's research uncovered that customers left larger tips to waitresses with certain physical characteristics, including being slender, being blonde, or having big boobs. Lynn defended his study as important because it could help potential waitresses gauge their "prospects in the industry."

Sentenced to sixty years in prison for the first-degree murder of a waitress in Washington, D.C.: **Gene Satan Downing.**

—*Washington Times*, December 5, 2001

Police in Round Rock, Texas, were dispatched to the Twin Peaks restaurant on a report of a waitress armed with an assault rifle. When the officers arrived they were met by five sheriff's deputies from Midland, nearly 350 miles away. Apparently, the visiting deputies had given the waitress, Vanda "Bambi" Purvis, an assault rifle so she could pose on the hood of one of their patrol cars. "We take a lot of pictures here, you know what I'm saying," said Sam Baiocco, manager of Twin Peaks, where waitresses are adorned in halter tops and short-shorts. According to an August 11, 2009, article in the *Austin American Statesman*, one of the Midland deputies was fired, three were suspended without pay, and the other was reprimanded. "At no point at any time was anyone in any danger because we took proper precaution," said Purvis. "Besides, I know how to use that gun."

W warnings

In the spirit of "love thy neighbor," two men living next door to each other decided to split the cost of yard work and purchased a brand-new Black & Decker gas-powered lawnmower together. Warmed in the glow of neighborly love, they decided it would be a great idea to use the lawnmower to trim the hedge that divided their property. So with one neighbor on his side of the hedge and the other neighbor on his they hoisted the lawnmower into the air and glided it across the top of the hedge. The mower blade snagged on the shrub and the resulting kickback caused serious injury to both men. Again working in tandem, both men decided to sue the manufacturer on the grounds that there was no warning on the lawnmower stating that it shouldn't be used as a hedge trimmer.

warnings

A group of men who competed in a foot race while carrying refrigerators on their backs sued the manufacturer because the appliances carried insufficient warnings of possible injury from such activity.

California requires a warning label on all packages that contain lead. This holds true for bullets. The warning reads "This product contains lead and may be hazardous to your health."

S ince 1997, Michigan Lawsuit Abuse Watch has published the winners of their "Wacky Warning Label Contest." Here are some of the highlights:

A label on a baby stroller: "Remove child before folding."

A brass fishing lure with a three-pronged hook on the end: "Harmful if swallowed."

A popular scooter for children: "This product moves when used."

A nine-by-three-inch bag of air used as packing material: "Do not use this product as a toy, pillow, or flotation device."

A flushable toilet brush: "Do not use for personal hygiene."

A digital thermometer that can be used to take a person's temperature several different ways: "Once used rectally, the thermometer should not be used orally."

A household iron: "Never iron clothes while they are being worn."

A label on a hair dryer: "Never use hair dryer while sleeping."

A warning on an electric drill made for carpenters: "This product not intended for use as a dental drill."

A *smoke detector:* "Do not use the Silence Feature in emergency situations. It will not extinguish a fire."

A *cardboard car sunshield that keeps sun off the dashboard:* "Do not drive with sunshield in place."

An *"Aim 'n Flame" fireplace lighter:* "Do not use near fire, flame, or sparks."

A label on a handheld massager advises consumers not to use "while sleeping or unconscious."

A *twelve-inch rack for storing compact discs:* "Do not use as a ladder."

A *cartridge for a laser printer:* "Do not eat toner."

A *thirteen-inch wheel on a wheelbarrow:* "Not intended for highway use."

A *can of self-defense pepper spray:* "May irritate eyes."

A *pair of shin guards manufactured for bicyclists:* "Shin pads cannot protect any part of the body they do not cover."

A *snowblower:* "Do not use on roof."

A *dishwasher:* "Do not allow children to play in the dishwasher."

A *popular manufactured fireplace log:* "Caution—Risk of Fire."

A *box of birthday cake candles:* "DO NOT use soft wax as ear plugs or for any other function that involves insertion into a body cavity."

warnings

W warrants

A Jefferson County, Alabama, sheriff's deputy was refueling her marked patrol car when twenty-seven-year-old Matthew Kinard pulled up next to her in his truck and asked her to check if police had any outstanding warrants against him. "I told him that I would, but if he had warrants I would have to arrest him," Sergeant Venita Edge said in her report. "The offender gave me his license and said he did not think he had warrants, but if so, to please not arrest him." Sure enough, there was a warrant for Kinard on drug charges and the deputy placed him under arrest. According to a September 15, 2010, article in the *North Jefferson News*, Kinard said in his defense, "I am the stupidest criminal in the world."

A man in Las Vegas was reading the local paper about a suspect who was wanted on several sexual assaults in the area. To his surprise, he noticed a striking resemblance between himself and the wanted man. It wasn't him, of course, but he wanted authorities to know he wasn't the one they were looking for. Police guaranteed the paranoid man he wasn't a suspect in the case but thanked him for doing his civic duty and dropping by the station. On a hunch the police ran the man's name through their computer and soon arrested him on an outstanding warrant from California on assault and drug charges.

Hey, the guy must have thought to himself, I may be a violent drug addict but I'm not a rapist.

warrants

The attorney for Christopher Plovie, who was on trial for drug possession in 1990, claimed his client had been illegally searched because the officers didn't have a warrant. In countering that claim, the prosecution stated the officer didn't need a warrant because a "bulge" in Plovie's jacket, which could have been a gun, gave the officer probable cause to search. Plovie, who was wearing the same jacket in the Pontiac, Michigan, court that day, was outraged. He handed the jacket to the judge to prove the material the jacket was made of simply didn't bulge. After examining the jacket, the judge reached into one of the pockets and pulled out a packet of cocaine.

weapons

Decai Liu of Broken Arrow, Oklahoma, was arrested and charged with assault with a dangerous weapon after beating his roommate over the head with a blunt instrument: a harmonica. According to an October 8, 2009, article in the *Tulsa World*, instead of facing the music when police were called to arrest him, Liu resisted arrest and head-butted one of the officers and had to be subdued with pepper spray. The harmonica was seized and taken in as evidence.

In Columbia, Missouri, a man failed in his attempt to rob a grocery store using a socket wrench as his only weapon.

W

weapons

A bank robber carrying a crossbow, an ax, a stun gun, a smoke grenade, and a can of Mace walked into a bank in Osaka, Japan, and declared a holdup. He told the frightened tellers he was prepared to use them all if they didn't come across with the money. Fearing for their lives, the clerks gave the man $1,120,000, which he grabbed and then attempted to make his escape. Unfortunately for the robber, but fortunately for the bank, the crook was so loaded down with weapons that he tripped and was quickly apprehended by a passerby. Too much of a good thing is a bad thing.

A robber using a manhole cover
as a weapon stole seventy-five dollars
from a Chicago man.

STUPID

"The carrying of concealed weapons is forbidden unless same are exhibited to public view."

—POCATELLO, IDAHO, LAW

They make a perfect sandwich but not necessarily perfect weapons. Police in Aachen, Germany, reported that two shoppers fighting over an empty cart in the parking lot of a supermarket escalated into a meat and cheese attack. A seventy-four-year-old man who was thwarted in his attempt to claim an empty shopping cart went into the store and attacked the thirty-five-year-old woman who had the cart with a hunk of salami. She retaliated by stabbing at him with a wedge of Parmesan cheese.

Three youthful robbers used a golf ball as a weapon to rob a bicyclist. One of the boys hit the bicyclist with the ball, knocking him off the bike. The other two stole his wallet.

Notorious criminals are given nicknames that match their heinous crimes: the Boston Strangler, Jack the Ripper, Son of Sam, and the Zucchini Bandit. Yep, the Zucchini Bandit. But we won't have to worry about this vegetable for a long time as he was sentenced to eighteen years to life in prison. Justice Randall Eng, who sentenced the man, declared, "You added to the climate of fear we have to live in." His crime? He held up a man and took twenty dollars and a watch, claiming he had a concealed weapon in his coat. The weapon turned out to be a zucchini. The victim probably wondered if the man really had a gun in his pocket or if he was just glad to see him.

A grocery store robbery in Calgary, Alberta, was hindered because of two things: 1) the robber's only weapon was an ordinary manual can opener, and 2) during the attempted getaway, the sixteen-month-old baby of the robber's girlfriend kept falling out of its stroller.

weird W

66"I know there is no excuse for my atrocious behavior, and I am truly sorry for what I did back then. I express my profound apologies to Asda and to its staff and customers," said thirty-year-old Adeel Ayub, a former employee at a British grocery store. Ayub was caught on videotape urinating into a trash bin, destroying awards earned by the store, slashing coworkers' clothing and staff room furniture, setting off fire extinguishers, and licking raw chickens that were returned to shelves. According to a January 20, 2010, article in the *Guardian*, Ayub, a resident of Preston, Lancashire, in England, was arrested for criminal damage and was sentenced by a Preston magistrate court to fifty-six days on each of the five counts, to run concurrently, according to a spokeswoman for the court.

Forty-eight-year-old Scott Bennett lost an eye in a fight at the Mavericks nightclub in Sioux City, Iowa, in July 2008, according to an October 14, 2008, article in the *Sioux City Journal*. Then, in another fight at the same nightclub on October 12, Bennett lost his other eye.

Timothy Placko was pulled over by police on a wooded road in Port St. Lucie, Florida. Inside his car, police found a blond wig, rope, binoculars, a small machete, knives, gloves, two bullet casings, and a film canister that contained eighteen human teeth. They also discovered, on the passenger's seat, a stack of women's sonograms that Placko claimed he had downloaded from the Internet. According a July 7, 2008, report on West Palm Beach television station WPEC-TV, Placko originally told police that he had pulled off the road to call a "girlfriend" and then later admitted he hadn't called anyone. He was charged with carrying a concealed weapon.

According to a May 8, 2008, article in the *Kansas City Star*, sixteen people had to undergo rabies treatment in Hilton Head, South Carolina, after being exposed to a baby raccoon later discovered to have rabies. According to hospital records, some of the sixteen possible victims claimed to have merely cuddled the infected animal while an undisclosed number admitted to kissing the raccoon on the lips.

An unidentified forty-six-year-old man in Eerbeek, Netherlands, reported to police that someone had stolen his collection of ecstasy pills. The man claimed he was neither a dealer nor a user but was afraid that someone might ingest some of the 2,400-pill collection that he had painstakingly acquired over twenty years. The man kept the pills in individual coin-collecting folders and was quoted as saying, "I've tried it before but didn't like it. My passion for collecting comes from the varied collection of colors, shapes, and logos that are printed on the pills." According to a December 13, 2009, Associated Press article, the man approached police not to get his collection back but to warn them that approximately forty of the pills were probably poisonous.

weird

W

According to a November 19, 2003, article in the *Sarasota Herald Tribune*, Judi Roberts, a resident of Sarasota, Florida, suffered a stroke in 1999 while doing a crossword puzzle. It paralyzed her right side and left her unable to speak. Over several years of intensive physical therapy, the woman regained control of her right side, and her speech slowly improved. But instead of her familiar New York accent, she now spoke with a very distinct British accent. The fifty-seven-year-old woman was diagnosed with "foreign accent syndrome." There have been fewer than twenty reported cases worldwide since 1919.

Doctors initially diagnosed a tumor when Brewster, Massachusetts, resident Ron Sveden's left lung collapsed. But according to a report on television station WHDH in Boston, doctors soon realized that Sveden had ingested a plant seed that somehow traveled into his lung and sprouted.

wienermobiles

S ince the attacks on the United States on
September 11, 2001, several roads near the
Pentagon have been closed to commercial traffic
(vehicles with six wheels or more) because of
the fear of truck bombs. So when police saw a
twenty-seven-foot-long vehicle cruising on the
road they jumped into action. The two occupants
of the car, Will Keller and Paula Pendleton, were
detained and questioned before eventually being
released. Officials were immediately suspicious
of the vehicle not only because it was on a
restricted road but because it was shaped like
a hot dog. Yep, it was the famous Oscar Mayer
Wienermobile that had got lost while traveling
through Washington on a yearlong charity drive.
"[The drivers of the Wienermobile] were very
apologetic," an Oscar Mayer spokeswoman said.
"They just did not realize. They were sorry for
any sort of traffic delay." Virginia State Police
spokeswoman Lucy Caldwell said, "Obviously,
this was a mistake. This hot dog posed no threat
to us."

W

wienermobiles

When Nick Krupp arrived at the lakefront house he was renting from his mother in Mount Pleasant, Wisconsin, he was surprised to see a new addition—the Oscar Mayer Wienermobile had crashed into the house. The two women driving the Wienermobile, code-named WEENR, had made a wrong turn onto a dead-end street and tried to turn the hot-rod hot dog around. But the driver hit the accelerator and smashed the super sausage into the garage and deck of the house, causing significant damage. According to a July 16, 2009, Associated Press article, the home is in a suburb of Racine just south of Franksville (no joke).

"WIENERMOBILE: CONTESTANTS RELISH THE THOUGHT"

—*Wisconsin State Journal*, June 1, 2004

"I've pulled out a lot of vehicles," said Dave Kurzejewski of Costy's Truck and Auto Mart. "But that's the first wiener I've ever pulled out." Kurzejewski was talking frankly about being called by Mansfield, New York, police to pull the stuck Oscar Mayer Wienermobile from a snow-covered highway. Emily Volpini and Caylen Goudie, the two hotdoggers who were driving the Wienermobile when it went off the road on February 10, 2008, were unhurt but did nearly freeze their buns off waiting for the tow truck in the cold weather.

W | wills

Donald Eugene Russell, an Oregon poet who died February 3, 1994, at sixty-four, was refused his last wish: to have the skin removed from his corpse so it could be tanned and used as binding for a volume of his poetry. On April 4, 1994, Rachel Barton-Russell, the poet's widow, settled with the state after they filed a lawsuit halting the request. She agreed to have him cremated instead.

Upon his death in 1995, chief justice of the United States Warren Burger left a will consisting of three sentences. It was so nonspecific and vague that it cost his heirs thousands of dollars in taxes.

In January 1995, Anna Morgan left her entire estate, valued at $500,000, to Tinker, her eleven-year-old Angora cat. As a condition of the will, Morgan's Seattle apartment was maintained through a trust fund that also hired a live-in caretaker to look after Tinker.

witnesses

W

Robert B. Bowling, a partner in the firm of Stumbo, Bowling, and Barber in Middlesboro, Kentucky, was questioning the wife of a man accused of resisting arrest and running from the police. Bowling was trying to prove that the police had used excessive force and that the defendant had escaped in order to protect himself. Bowling's exchange with the defendant's wife went like this:

Bowling: "Do you believe the police officers were abusive or rough with your husband?"

Witness: "Yeah, they were slinging him around so he broke and run."

Bowling: "What happened next?"

Witness: "The policeman asked me [my husband's] name and I told him I didn't know."

Bowling: "What happened after that?"

Witness: "The police called me a fat, lying whore."

Bowling: "What did you say to that?"

Witness: "I told him I ain't no liar."

W

In a Houston, Texas, courtroom in April 1994, Arthur Hollingsworth was on trial for the armed robbery of a convenience store. Hollingsworth waived his constitutional right to remain silent and testified in his own defense. Harris County prosecutor Jay Hileman eventually got Hollingsworth to admit that he was, in fact, in the Sun Mart convenience store at the time of the holdup. Hileman then got Hollingsworth to admit he had taken a gun into the store with him at the time it was robbed. Hileman then moved in for the kill.

Hileman: "Mr. Hollingsworth, you're guilty, aren't you?"

Hollingsworth: "No."

Hileman: "Mr. Hollingsworth, you're guilty, aren't you?"

Hollingsworth: "Yeah."

Prosecutor Hileman was stunned. "I couldn't believe it," he said. "I quit after that." When Hollingsworth's trial resumed the following day, the jury, because of his lack of a criminal record, or his amazing honesty, gave the convicted robber only five years in prison. They could have given him life.

wood chippers

In 2001, a forty-three-year-old Canadian woman left a four-page suicide note before diving into a wood chipper on her family's acreage near Ottawa.

It must have been both the best and worst day of her life after a young Phoenix, Arizona, woman accepted a marriage proposal from her twenty-year-old boyfriend. The man, who worked at a landscaping business, asked her if she would go with him to his work site in August 2000—and she accepted this second proposal as well. Once at the work site he took her hand and led her over to a wood chipper and turned it on. Before she knew what was happening, the man, whose hand she had just accepted in holy matrimony, climbed into the chipper and was using that same hand to pull her into the machine. She quickly turned into the runaway bride and escaped while her fiancé simply went to pieces.

W

Josh Thompson was thirteen feet up a ladder when he saw a man who had been lurking around his work site run toward a still-running wood chipper. Thompson saw what the man was about to do and leaped to the ground and hit the kill switch on the tree trimmer, which can grind up a twenty-one-inch tree trunk in seconds. The machine was winding down as the unnamed twenty-year-old man leaped in headfirst, catching and mangling his arm in the machine. "A split second later, and it would've been over," said a spokesman for the tree service. According to a May 17, 2008, *St. Paul Pioneer Press* article, a witness to the attempted suicide asked, "Have you ever seen the movie *Fargo*?"

xenophobia X

"You cannot go to a 7-Eleven or a
Dunkin' Donuts unless you have a slight
Indian accent. . . . I'm not joking."

—Senator Joe Biden (D-DE) on the C-SPAN series
Road to the White House, June 17, 2006

During the World Cup soccer competition in
1994, Addison, Texas, city officials warned
restaurant owners to be wary of possible credit
card fraud perpetrated by Nigerians who came
to support their soccer team. Councilman Dick
Wilke said restaurant owners should inform
the police "if thirty people come in speaking
Nigerian." There's only one problem with this
level of alertness: There is no such language as
Nigerian; the country's official language is English.

X

xenophobia

"Why do they kill people of other religions because of religion? Why do they hate the Israelis and despise their right to exist? Why do they hate each other? Why do Sunnis kill Shiites? How do they tell the difference? They all look the same to me."

—Senator Trent Lott (R-MS), explaining why he isn't in charge of U.S. foreign policy, September 28, 2006

x-rays

An unidentified Taiwanese man who suffered from a severe dry cough for many years and who could find no relief from either Western or Chinese medicine finally had an X-ray performed. A doctor, Chiou Ming-hwang, director of the respiratory center at Cathay General Hospital in Taipei, spotted the trouble: a sewing needle was lodged deep in the man's back nearly pricking his lung. The man claimed to have no memory of being stuck with a needle, but the man's wife recalled losing one several years earlier in their bed.

x-rays

A newlywed couple from Massachusetts, Mark and Hillary Meltz, were finally able to relax and enjoy their Hawaiian honeymoon safe in the knowledge that their wedding ring had been "returned." Mark had left the wedding ring on a counter but when he went back to get it, it was gone. Mark checked with Hillary and his brother, but no one knew where the ring had gone. It was soon discovered that the couple's Labrador, Liza, had retrieved it and an X-ray confirmed the new location of the ring.

On the day of their wedding Mark presented Hillary with an X-ray of the dog's stomach that showed the unmistakable image of the ring. Fortunately, she laughed instead of cried and they were pronounced man and wife. Mark's parents told the couple to go on their honeymoon and that they would watch the dog—at both ends. After the parents loaded the dog up with treats, Liza vomited and the ring came clinking out. I suppose this makes the ring a little more bearable to wear as opposed to the other way it could have come out.

Six-year-old Steven Varley was trying to keep a quarter away from his eight-year-old brother, Ian. Since Ian was bigger, Steven thought the best place to hide the quarter was in his mouth. So Steven put his money where his mouth, but the quarter had another idea—it slipped down into this throat. Steven's mother, Karen, grabbed the phone and called 911. "Hi. This is Karen Varley. My six-year-old has a quarter stuck in his throat, lodged in his throat," Varley said.

"Is he able to breathe?" a dispatcher asked.

"A little bit, yes," Varley replied. The dispatcher gave the mother instructions on how to handle the situation. Paramedics arrived and took Steven to the hospital, where he was X-rayed. The doctors received the quarter, and other things, when the boy threw up.

yugoslavia

Lidové Noviny, a newspaper from the Czech Republic, reported on May 13, 2009, that, as late as 1975, the Communist government of Czechoslovakia was actively planning to dig a very long tunnel to use for a rail line. The tunnel would go from their landlocked country underneath Austria and the part of Yugoslavia that is now Slovenia, all the way to the Adriatic Sea, 250 miles away. It is not known whether the country sought permission to dig under these two independent countries or even what the Austrians and the Yugoslavs thought of the idea.

A sign in a former Yugoslavian hotel reads
**"The flattening of underwear with pleasure
is the job of the chambermaid."**

The Gorani, a small Muslim ethnic group scattered through the former Socialist Federal Republic of Yugoslavia (primarily in present-day Serbia, Kosovo, Macedonia, and Albania), didn't fight for a nation-state to call their own; they just wanted enough freedom to practice their cultural traditions—such as one called "Sunet." Every five years, Goranis gather in southern Kosovo for a festival of mass circumcision of young boys. In 2007, 130 boys, ranging from ten months to five years old, were circumcised by seventy-year-old Zylfikar Shishko, a barber from the town of Prizren who has been performing the role for the last forty-five years. According to an October 17, 2008, report from Spiegel Online, many Goranis are concerned about 2012—not because it's the end of the Mayan calendar, but because Shishko is the only skilled Gorani circumciser.

Y | yule

Every year in the Swedish city of Gävle, the oldest city in Sweden's historical Northern Lands (Norrland), Swedes filled with Christmas cheer celebrate by building a gigantic straw Yule Goat. And every year, Christmas Scrooge Swedes respond by burning the highly combustible icon to the ground. According to a December 25, 2009, article in the *San Francisco Chronicle*, the first Yule Goat was built in 1966 and was quickly followed by the first burning of the Yule Goat. On occasions the Yule Goat has also been shredded, amputated, and mutilated before being torched.

The Caga Tió is a fixture in Spanish Christmas traditions and can be equated to a slightly perverted piñata. Caga Tió, which translates to "pooping log," is a small log with a drawn or applied face, little legs, and usually a cape of some kind. In early December, the adults in a household will "feed" the log by putting in small treats such as hazelnuts or small pieces of chocolate. Then, on Christmas Day, the children joyously gather around the Caga Tió and beat it with sticks until it drops its load through a small hole in its underside. On December 25, 2009, the *San Francisco Chronicle* featured a traditional song that accompanies the beating of the Caga Tió:

> Poop turrón [sweet nougat candy],
> Hazelnuts and cottage cheese,
> If you don't poop well,
> I'll hit you with a stick,
> Poop log!
> Poop log!
> Log of Christmas,
> Don't poop herrings,
> Which are too salty,
> Poop turrón
> Which is much better!

zero tolerance

Seventeen-year-old Matthew Whalen, a senior at Troy, New York's Lansingburgh High School, is an honors student, an Eagle Scout, and wants to attend the U.S. Military Academy at West Point. Whalen, who had recently completed an army basic training course and serves in the National Guard, was confronted by school officials who had learned that he was known to carry a knife. He told them that the only knife he has is one with a 1 1/2-inch blade in a survival pack that he keeps in his car.

"They asked me to show it to them," Whalen said. "I didn't realize it was going to be a problem. I knew it wasn't illegal—my police chief grandfather gave the knife to me." His car was in the school's parking lot, and "the principal even admitted that I had no intent to use the knife, that I had no accessibility to the knife," but Whalen was still suspended for "possession" of a "weapon" on campus in accordance with the school's zero-tolerance policy. According to an October 14, 2009, article on the Huffington Post, following a district superintendent review of his five-day suspension, it was boosted to twenty days. "He's lucky that he didn't have a bayonet in the car," said his police chief grandfather. "He's a National Guardsman for God's sake."

Z

zero
tolerance

A thirteen-year-old Portland, Oregon, student was suspended for a week because he violated the schools zero-tolerance policy on alcohol. The boy was caught swallowing some Scope mouthwash because "the lunch kind of tasted bad. I didn't have any place to spit."

A nine-year-old student from Weems Elementary School in Manassas, Virginia, was suspended under the school's zero-tolerance policy on drugs. The boy had been caught giving his friends a Certs breath mint. The school policy not only bans real drugs but also "look-alikes" that a reasonable person would believe is a controlled substance. Defending his son's reputation, the boy's father said, "He's not a breath-mint addict or anything like that." Not yet, but who knows where something like this might lead.

Citing the school's "zero-tolerance sexual harassment policy," administrators at McElwain Elementary School in Thornton, Colorado, threatened to suspend a ten-year-old girl for repeatedly asking one boy if he liked her and her friends.

zero tolerance

A thirteen-year-old girl who suffers from acute asthma began having an asthma attack on the school bus ride home. She didn't have her inhaler with her and her breathing was becoming more and more labored. A quick-thinking friend, who also has asthma, reached into her bag and pulled out her own inhaler and gave it to her classmate. Both of the girls' mothers considered the act to be heroic and worthy of an award. But school officials, citing their zero-tolerance policy against drugs, have labeled the girl who handed over her inhaler a "drug trafficker." It is a notation that will stay on her school record for three years. Zero tolerance for the heroic schoolgirl—zero intelligence for the school board. I don't know about you, but that decision leaves me breathless.